CACOPHONY

CACOPHONY

RUBY WEI

NDP

NEW DEGREE PRESS

COPYRIGHT © 2021 RUBY WEI

All rights reserved.

CACOPHONY

ISBN 978-1-63730-827-1 *Paperback*
      978-1-63730-889-9 *Kindle Ebook*
      978-1-63730-961-2 *Ebook*

"此情可待成追忆 只是当时已惘然"

——李商隐·《锦瑟》

"人生如梦,一樽还酹江月"

——苏轼·《念奴娇》

National Human Trafficking Hotline: Call 1-888-373-7888 (TTY: 711) or *Text 233733

写给我爸爸妈妈

我一生都仰慕你们
这本书离不开你们对我的爱

contents

AUTHOR'S NOTE		1
PROLOGUE		7
MOMENTARY SNAPSHOTS		11
CHAPTER 1.	DAMN STRAIGHT, RIGHT INTO HIS BALLS	21
CHAPTER 2.	IF I CALLED WEBSTER WOULD HE ANSWER?	25
CHAPTER 3.	WHITE FLOWER WILTS	29
CHAPTER 4.	NORMAL SUITS YOU NOT	39
CHAPTER 5.	HE'S A TURD	49
CHAPTER 6.	FESTERING SORE	53
CHAPTER 7.	MY DAUGHTER, GO MAKE SOMETHING OF YOURSELF	59
CHAPTER 8.	A MEA CULPA	65
CHAPTER 9.	HE JUST LOOKS LIKE A WASTE OF SPACE	73
CHAPTER 10.	I NEED MORE TIME	77

CHAPTER 11.	I'M A FROG	89
CHAPTER 12.	HUMANITY	95
CHAPTER 13.	HE GOT ME	105
CHAPTER 14.	NO SIR WE ARE NOT DOING THIS	109
CHAPTER 15.	THE WOMAN WHO WOULD NOT STOP STARING	123
CHAPTER 16.	ON AUTHENTICITY	127
CHAPTER 17.	DÉJÀ VU	135
CHAPTER 18.	HOW MANY MORE	141
CHAPTER 19.	EXPLOSION OF STARS	145
CHAPTER 20.	ZEUS PLEASE, JUST GO	147
CHAPTER 21.	ET TU BRUTE	159
CHAPTER 22.	IDIOCY	163
CHAPTER 23.	LULLABY-LIKE PARITTAS	165
CHAPTER 24.	YOU CAN'T HAVE ME	167
CHAPTER 25.	WELCOME	179
CHAPTER 26.	DEATH IS EASY	183
CHAPTER 27.	I WAS TOO LATE	195
CHAPTER 28.	KANGBASHI	199
CHAPTER 29.	DA-DUM-DA-DUM-DA-DUM	205
CHAPTER 30.	ON NOT BELONGING	209
CHAPTER 31.	I PROMISE	215
CHAPTER 32.	YOU'LL BE SAFE	223

CHAPTER 33. SHE SAID NOTHING	227
CHAPTER 34. AVICI	235
CHAPTER 35. INCHOATE VIGNETTES	243
CHAPTER 36. MR. JIM RALEIGH	261
CHAPTER 37. FREE	265
EPILOGUE	273
ACKNOWLEDGMENTS	275

author's note

―

a note from me to you:

You, my reader, are everything to me.

Thank you for opening this book. You have a million other things to do, and you so graciously chose to flip open *this* cover. I sincerely cannot thank you enough to express how I feel, so I'll save my publisher some ink and end it with: eternally grateful. That, I am and forever will be. And I am enchanted to meet you …

At its core, *Cacophony* is a story from my heart and all the things I care about. Issues I follow, my insecurities, longings, sources of happiness, the things that make me stay up all night talking to my best friends, and ceaseless questions can all be found within these pages. Essentially, I put everything I have, my soul and my essence, into a time capsule to hand to you. Writing this made me feel alive in ways nothing else could. I hope it evokes something in you, too. *Cacophony* is something I'd pick up at the end of a long week, pour a glass of chilled white wine, light a clean-scented candle with a pretty name like "Midsummer's Night," and simply hang out with. *Hygge. Lagom. Mys.* The Danes and Swedes encapsulate the ambiance of coziness using these words.

I will be closing out the happiest year of my life by the time *Cacophony* is released. This entire period of time, I was happy. Happy in the sense that I was in love with life, not happy in the sense that everything was going the way I wanted. Because it wasn't. In fact, some of my best days were days when everything that could possibly go wrong went ahead and decided to go wrong together. They're my dramatic stories, my heartiest laughs, my loveliest memories.

In this year, I lived utterly unapologetically. I don't know why I hadn't tried living like this before, but it certainly suits me well. In this year, I toned down the lifetime of insecurities bogging me down, keeping me awake in the darkest of nights, and wholeheartedly tuned in with that part of myself I can't help but fall deeper and deeper in love with. In this year, I listened to my heart more often than I ever have before—I individually picked out the cacophony of voices that was drowning it out, shut them down, and allowed my heart to ring loud and clear. Make no mistake, I think this caused more problems for me than the solutions it solved, but I have never been happier with myself. In my universe, happiness and creativity tread hand in hand.

If parallel universes do indeed exist, I always thought the only way to access them in my lifetime is to be immersed in a good story. Letting yourself be absorbed in a story allows you to love all of humanity—all the terrible, despicable failures it contains, as well as all the beautiful, wonderful miracles it embodies. This experience creates such a sense of empathy. I convinced myself that empathy is the theme of *Cacophony*, but I also know I could easily say that's the theme of every book I write after this, for it's an absolute aspiration of mine. Empathy, kindness, and honesty.

I wanted to include a Sparknotes-esque Easter egg for you to differentiate the empathy I mean to explore in this novel from the rest of my books that do not currently exist but will: you will never find a single literal physical description of Idalia in the entire book.

You will never know the color of her eyes or how long her hair is because she is crafted like a dream. Is life nothing but a dream? Are we drifting through stage, merely playing our parts? Or are we going impromptu, ceaselessly trying to create a legacy that is of our own, all the while believing there is nothing new under the sun? Or have we taken the initiative to hop off stage, to become our own audience?

I don't know. Do you?

I took inspiration from *Dream of the Red Chamber*, a great legend in Chinese literature. Professors have dedicated their entire lives to studying this one book if that puts its legacy in perspective for you. To be honest, I couldn't make it through. I might try again soon; I might take a class. As of now, I got through maybe eleven chapters. Out of 120. I've never read anything more confusing; not even Shakespeare lifted my brain out of my head the way this book did. In *Cacophony*, contrasting Idalia's ethereal presence with Dolkar's vivid imagery is meant to say: at the border of dreams and pain is a line of unity. As much as Dolkar's vulnerability, which brought her to her worst, is not her fault, none of the building blocks that instigated Idalia's rose-tinted view of the world, which shields her from the worst, are her fault. In this juxtaposition, there is more than enough space for kindness. If we listen to understand instead of listening to reply, perhaps it could be the beginning of the collapse of some of our prejudice and pride, our hatred and hostility.

I will be on the threshold of venturing toward a career I absolutely am in love with by the time *Cacophony* is released. I hope to be loving my job as much as I loved writing this book. Love, I do not use lightly. I am not *a* hopeless romantic—I am just hopelessly romantic. I love within seconds, deeply and irrevocably: from the way Monet painted his water lilies by chasing the iridescent light; to the way the sun—in explosions of brilliancy and beauty—set beyond Volcán Tolimán right as I dived into the depths of Lake Atitlán, so mesmerized by it I almost forgot to climb out when lightning struck; to the way Margaret Mitchell crafted Scarlett's stubborn nature in *Gone with the Wind* and how freakishly accurate it is to my own; to the way Van Gogh depicted the poorest cottages and the dirtiest corners with irresistible charm; to the way my mom and grandma sound in their mellifluous Sichuan dialect, each sentence rising and falling in various ways, effortlessly melodic; to my dad's ability to roast all my shortcomings mercilessly, a candid expression of his love, I now understand; to the sounds of languages I cannot comprehend; to the moment my life was saved in Ecuador in an event I can only fathom as divine intervention—indeed, I even ended up falling in love with that moment if only by reasons of it affirming my faith to me.

Ironically, I have never been *in* love with anyone—in my world, it just has to *happen*. I cannot expect it; I don't want to be expecting it.

In the same way I romanticize life and love, I fell in love with *Cacophony*: abruptly, impulsively, and fiercely at first—slowly hesitating because fear was stronger than infatuation and the fear of vulnerability more powerful than confidence in what I had to say—then suddenly all at once. Initially, everything about the idea of becoming an author intrigued me. An *author*. Even that word brings a sparkle to my eyes. I wanted to be one so bad, not knowing what it entailed. And then I started writing.

In the early stages, this story felt dead to me. But I never stopped letting myself *feel* for things, *feel* for people, *feel* for issues going on in our world; I never stopped allowing my heart to be broken for the world. When it reached a point when the story became *so much more* than myself, when it started to explore empathy through the lens of minorities from different nations, when it became an Asian-American narrative that stands on its own, that's when I truly started believing in it.

Still, it drove me crazy more often than not.

There were days I sat and stared at my screen, waiting for inspiration like it was about to come and bonk me on the head any minute. I was disappointed when that did not work; I was talking to inspiration like a mad woman. I sat at the grave site of Hans Christian Andersen, Danish master of fairy tales, hoping his spirit would enlighten me, like an even madder woman.

There were days I hated writing because everything came out wrong, and grand ideas that seemed so limitless in my head came through in words that shrunk them to nothing, no bigger than the words on a menu in a café you glance at for two seconds before getting the same drink you get every time. And one mundane day, I just woke up realizing how strongly I'd already started to identify with "author," how it has magnified my ordinary life and spun it into ethereal eunoia, how deeply I need it to feel alive. I am in love, I thought, skipping down the streets of Copenhagen.

There is a feeling the French call *énouement*, a bittersweetness we feel when we can't go back and tell our past selves what we know now. I think it's a beautiful feeling, fully identified only when we let ourselves dwell in it for a little while. Writing gave me the excuse to dwell in it a little longer than I should have, but I hope you will fill up the deep chasms I have left open with your own thoughts and curiosities.

I did not intentionally leave such chasms; they are there because no story is really complete, or so I believe. There's always greater infinities within the limited timelines that invite us to sprinkle life into. And how do we sprinkle life onto fragile ideas brought out by twenty-six letters, some dots, and some dots with tails attached to them?

We live.

There is a feeling the Germans call *fernweh*, which is the notion of missing a place we have never been. I've had harsh symptoms of *fernweh* more times than I can count, each case heavier than the last. I miss those places because I *have* been. I went to Kenya and ran into a pride of lions on a safari ride … through the eyes of Shumin, a retired doctor—now author. Through the eyes of Sanmao, I went to the Sahara and lived with Sahrawi people, witnessing a wedding with horror when a groom violently took the ten-year-old bride's virginity with all the wedding guests standing by, listening, and cheering; it's custom, they told me, she's supposed to scream like that. Between the space where I long to be a thousand different people, live a million different lives, I sprinkle my own life into. My world has since expanded.

In Greek, to leave a piece of yourself in your work is termed *meraki*. Myself, I leave with you.

And in my own language, 缘分 (*yuanfen*) is a destiny that brings people together. 缘分 brought us together in *Cacophony*.

Encantada, my friend. I hope you enjoy.

prologue

Time is warped. Much like our perceptions and our prejudice …

Dolkar

pg. 5

this obsidian-colored pen draws the one thin line
    keeping me here, alive—
alive when all i want is
not to be
alive
alive when all i thought i've ever been is
trash
alive when everything i've ever felt is
worthless

so what's the point of staying alive when—
when death isn't even an option

when your mere existence numbs you to the core
when you can't seem to—
to feel anything

for he sold me a dream
everything i've ever wanted, right there in front of me
so close i could nearly grasp it
and i—
i did the thing anyone else would
i
believed him
i
believed
him.

Idalia

"I had already bought our tickets," he smiled, a smile that never reached his eyes, as he pulled out two wrinkled, blotched tickets, torn apart and taped back together.

It was a promise he made that I really thought was a joke. I had long forgotten it was my dream. I had long forgotten *how* to dream.

I lowered my eyes, unable to look into his, afraid of what I'd see in them. I was standing in front of the hospital bed, forcing myself to nod, forcing back my tears, willing myself to stop breathing—I'd rather die than cry in front of him right then.

In that time of silence, it felt like not just one, or two, but three infinite lifetimes had passed between us.

In the first, our lives never would've crossed. Strangers we would've stayed. I wondered if I'd rather live in a world where we never met.

In the second, Walt Disney himself drafted every scene for our story. I wondered if God would publish that draft.

The third is now. This life.

Eventually, I choked out that I don't deserve it. It was so soft, I don't know if he heard. My already broken heart took the next three seconds to disintegrate into nothing.

I'm sorry. Between my love and myself, I chose myself.
I'm sorry. Between sacrifice and freedom, I chose freedom.
I'm sorry. Between him and family, I chose my family.

Within my short life, I've been loved through all of it. I've been the receiver of many sacrifices, some I ignorantly took for granted. I've also felt inadequate through most of that life; if sacrifice and what I made out of the sacrifices I was given were measurable and by the same scale, I wish I tipped the scale by working harder because to those whom much is given, much is expected. To try to live up to that love, I always tried to hold everything so tightly within my grasp.

The first time someone showed me how to be free, how to live my life according to my own standards, how to allow myself to love, all I gave him in return was a "happy birthday" and a bottle of Pinot Noir along with the white magnolias I left out to die.

Arno

pg. 3

the skinny, battered and broken girl I saw at
    the marketplace
the pain in her eyes
matched the pain I once saw in mine...
I can't get her off my mind
don't know why—I just can't
I'm not leaving until I figure out what's going
    on because
if not me, who?
if not now, when?

momentary snapshots

Dolkar

My mother-in-law looks at me the same way she looks at the five pigs she owns out back; six—one of them had a tiny gray piglet recently. In this village, where agriculture keeps things going and investment in its infrastructure is as close as the US is to breaking its duopoly, being viewed as worth something is not next to nothing.

"You did this on purpose!" Xiu screamed, immediately pouring a bucket of water onto the relentless flame without thinking.

"No!" I cried, jumping in to stymie the water using my hands. Unfortunately, though, water is the type of compound fingers do not stop.

"What!" Xiu yelped.

"Mother, do *not* pour water onto a grease fire," I gasped, grasping Xiu's elbow, realizing it was already too late: as the water made contact, the fire exploded like a snake turning into a dragon, eliciting a sharp shriek from my mother-in-law.

"What to do! What to do! You only do harm, no good, no good!" my mother-in-law yelled, flailing her arms and running in circles back and forth around the house as the flame only grew bigger.

I had forgotten how it even started—one second I had oil heating up in the pan while I bent down to chop a few cloves of garlic, the next second, the pot erupted. Just like that—BAM. SHAZAM. And this flame was indeed a stubborn one—it fought like an ox. I grabbed the gigantic towel with orange sunflowers on it, and weakly, with T. rex arms, sprawled it across this ox. The flame smothered for a few seconds, during which I was able to let out one long-held-in breath, before erupting again.

"What to do! What to do! You are a curse to this family!" Xiu continued hollering, solving nothing.

I grabbed another gigantic towel, this one with an emerald smiley face, dunked it in the waterlogged bowl of potatoes I was getting ready to wash, flung it onto the flame, finally choking it to ashes. I breathed out a long sigh of relief as I noticed my hands had been shaking. I wanted to cry and laugh at the same time.

"What to do! What to do! You will be the death of all of us!" Xiu continued, panting, still making laps around the coffee table in our tiny living room.

"Mother, it's out," I sighed.

"Oh."

The sink was burnt charcoal up to the rims, the pot was obviously ruined to smithereens, but all was good with the world. All was at peace again.

"You clumsy fool. Remind me to apply for your burial plot soon." Xiu rolled her eyes.

Well *that's* the last thing I needed.

Idalia

Historically named Zijincheng—where a glamorous palace situates itself, with grand walls built on top of the lives, blood, sweat, and tears of countless lost souls—this place was the former home of twenty-four emperors. Strolling through Zijincheng, packed to its throat with history and culture at every twist and turn, I imagined I was a theatre actress back in the Ming dynasty who got my start in Shanghai. Government officials from all over the dynasty hired me to perform—I was altogether dedicated to my art.

Then one day, after my name was already established throughout the kingdom, I was invited to perform at the palace by the emperor's personal decree. I hesitated; entangling myself with the royals would ultimately mean death for me because to describe them as ruthless would be a ridiculous understatement. If I was the one to step in front of their path to success (namely, the attention of the emperor), they would hesitate at *nothing* to eat me alive. Yet no one disobeyed this decree. Absolutely no one.

It was death one way or the other, just a matter of time. In the harem, where survival and upward mobility were dependent on the recognition of the emperor, going against their moral compass might become the optimal choice for many women. No woman outside the harem who wants to continue living would try to attract the attention of the emperor because you would not only have an empress consort against you, but the entire concubine force. You do not succeed against their malicious competition; they fight each other all the time, but with their eyes on you, they will coalesce their forces; they battle you as one because you are free, and they are not. If one of them doesn't kill you, another one will. They got how to get away with murder down to a tee. You do not win. You go to the emperor. You make him fall in love with you, for the only thing that could save you is his attention. It's either that, or you die.

"Yo, did you hear me?" Zion asked.

I blinked, and my little brother's face came into focus. "What?" Oh, right. Twenty-first century. We were in Beijing on a family vacation after I graduated high school.

"I said, do you want ice cream?" He emphasized each word slowly.

"Always. Get me the matcha one?"

"Sure."

Zion's gangly frame skipped over the cobblestones past a white bridge carved with exquisite dragons. The sun wasn't even directly overhead yet and the day was already hot. I watched Zion and my mom gather around the ice cream stand as I waited at the back of a long line of tourists getting ready to head inside the first main building—the Hall of Supreme Harmony—of the Forbidden City, a palace turned museum.

"Wait, just kidding, Mom says you can't have one." He ran back to me, nearly dropping the cone in his hand.

"What? I'm eighteen. I can't have ice cream?" I complained, hearing Legend, my older brother, and my dad chuckling behind me.

"She said it's too cold for you. Only you. Want a lick of mine?"

Putain. In Asian culture, consuming anything cold on your period is akin to smoking. Within those two days, my mom would rather see me doing that than eating ice cream.

"You need to fold up your umbrellas at this point," the security guard told everyone in line as we merged together to pass through security. From the looks of it, out of the sea of people in line, almost every female, age ten to fifty, had one propped up. Clear skies, eighty-five degrees, zero chance of rain.

"If I get darker, it's your fault. Pay me my white skin," the dainty girl ahead of me whined loudly.

I rolled my eyes. *Because only white is beautiful?* I thought, slathering my own skin in sunscreen.

You propeller of this stupid system. You're stupid. I'm stupid. We're all stupid. How lovely.

Clearly, I was in the right mood for a culture-seeking vacation. Not only did I wake up mad for no reason whatsoever, I'd never encountered a security guard who flipped through my journal before. At the security checkpoint of our first stop that day, Tiananmen Square, the security guard did just that. He flipped *through* the pages of my travel diary, as if me and my corrupt democratic ideals had the potential to threaten the nation. Who knows, it might. What? Are they going to send tanks after me as well?

I slightly wrinkled my brows and looked at the security guard, itching to ask why but not wanting to stop up the line; he answered me with a blank expression that said: this is protocol. Right. Protocol. The same type of protocol that killed hundreds, or thousands, or tens of thousands (who actually knows?) in the 1989 Tiananmen Massacre, the largest political protest for democracy in Communist Chinese history. Mao is currently clinking glasses with Xi from his grave, laughing at us plebs.

Throughout the day, every time I wanted to drink in the magic of these palaces, Zion kept complaining he was walking for hours to see a pot. Granted, they were these big water vats that looked like humongous, rounded out stock pots scattered throughout the museum, used to extinguish fires before fire stations existed. Never mind that it'd be worth 1,500 taels of silver per "pot" in the currency of the time, or 300,000 RMB, approximately $46,358 USD when I searched up the conversion rate that day.

"I agree. Why can't we stay home and stare at our cooking pots?" Legend clapped Zion on the back every time he complained.

"What looks like a pot to you? These walls of history or these stories of gold?" our parents scolded in unison. Never mind the Meridian Gate, a massive gate where emperors stood to announce their edict, the imperial garden, carefully sculpted in an evergreen landscape, the exquisite exhibitions; the only thing that stood out to their son was a pot.

As our tour wrapped up to a close, we passed a professional photo station where people were lining up to take pictures dressed up as emperors, empress consorts, princes, and princesses.

I glanced into it a second too long; a photographer leaning by, resting, asked, "Hey do you want to come in and try on the princess costume?"

"No, thank you." I smiled politely.

"For you, to try it is free," he urged.

"Actually, give me the emperor's," I declared fiercely, looking him straight in the eye, holding my chin up high, thinking back to my fantasy—what if I had been on the throne like Wu Zetian, the only female de facto leader in Chinese history, instead of receiving the decree from the emperor?

"Uh ... okay, little girl," he uttered.

My dad came over, asked for the price, immediately said, "No thank you," and turned around to leave. Fantasy cloud, poof, gone.

"Wait, dad—let me just try it."

"You think you could try it without paying?"

"But they *said* it was free to try on."

"Then how are they going to do business? Does this look like charity to you?"

"But I can just say I don't want the picture."

"You must be so pretty—you must be the *one* person they've waited all day to make an exception for."

My mom laughed. "My daughter, my genes, course she is."

My dad sighed. "Yup, basically a clone of you—none of me. Especially that common sense of hers, it's like I had no part in it."

Legend butted in with, "Stupid girl, I can find you an emperor's costume on Taobao for a hundred renminbi. Sixteen dollars."

"*Wow*, my family hates me," I mumbled, pouting, walking alongside four people all sucking on ice cream cones without me. Zion got the *matcha* one.

"Can I have a lick of that?" I begged.

They all laughed.

Golden hour illuminating our faces, strolling down the majestic steps, our laughter blended together into the soft evening and in that moment, right then and there, all was right and just and good in the world. No video camera in the universe could transcribe the beauty of that simple moment.

Dolkar

There's an old, abandoned, worn-down building in our village where a few old people gather sometimes. I didn't know who they were worshiping, or why. I heard snatches of what was supposed to be music, but that's all.

Back when I was in school, years ago, no one at home forced me to study. I'd spend all my evenings reading novels at the bookstore across my school, then I'd start cramming for the final at the end of the year, for fear I'd be hit on the hand by my teacher with that tan, wooden ruler if I failed again.

This morning, my mother-in-law screamed at me to chase back the piglet that ran away through a hole in the pig pen. The day was hazy, I didn't know where to start looking, but I saw clearly the origin of the sounds I heard every week as I peered into the window of that worn down building. A circle of old folks, ranging from sixty to eighty. Their lips moved slowly, yet together. Seeing this image, all I could think was that they're probably cramming for their final as well.

Idalia

pg. 16

i am confident
at least i could act the part
that as it may,
only
around you
oh God i became a nervous wreck
and for what?

Arno

I crave danger and I crave thrill. At first I was fairly mild. I mean, how reckless could I be at three? You know what,

I take that back. You'd be surprised. It was the bikes and scooters—the faster I went, the louder I laughed. I climbed trees, jumping from branch to branch like a monkey. No need to bring up the time I fell off and hit my head. I was fine. Momma was not. Not only did I almost send her to the hospital with a heart attack, a bill of $1,100 for my medical care was sent to her afterwards—there was a higher chance of me dying from her glare than the actual fall. I jumped fences, imagining robbers coming after me. One time I jumped in a pool because I thought I could swim—I couldn't. Not without arm floats, anyways.

Then I started realizing it for myself: it began with my first roller coaster at four, Sea World, and amusement parks; I upped my game around six or ten: Disney, water parks, Six Flags; sports: football, soccer, track and field. The exhilaration and the adrenaline sucked me in until I cared too much for my own good. I cared so much I took the fun out of it and scores started backfiring.

After I tore my ACL, for a while I couldn't compete. That summer, I traveled: hiking was always a blast; surfing, sailing, and bungee jumping hyped me up.

When we couldn't afford any of the traveling anymore, I was still seeking danger, still looking for wilderness. You know why? Because at the threshold of death, when every cell evoking your fight or flight response is telling you "Stop what you're about to do, you'll die," suddenly your life becomes clear to you: what's important, what you'd sacrifice for, your bottom line; the trade-offs for the things you think you want versus what you really want comes down to a few grand beliefs. The few beliefs branch off to a few mixed emotions that, with time, inspire you to *do* something different, *to be someone different.*

Idalia

pg. 26

I see him everywhere
he has infused himself into my worldview
without ever trying to and
I think that's beautiful because
he expanded it—
boy, he expanded my mind!

damn straight, right into his balls

Arno

Flash forward: two years later

Had I attempted this in America, I would've been shot. Picture the Wild West, cowboys and horses and Texas Rangers from back in the day. They would've shot me the second I barged in. Okay fine, tarnish that picture, smear some dust on it, think Homestead Act era.

Each step I took exhausted me more, dehydrated me further. "I need water," I croaked to a nearby armadillo and six vultures finishing off something I couldn't recognize. Raccoon, maybe. If it wasn't for the kind little boy who gave me a meal and water six hours ago, it would be me they were finishing off. The land was cracking for want of water itself, and wind caked everything my eyes could see in a red-brown tint. There was one road—the one I was staggering on, careful not to fall into any cacti. The broad-brimmed Stetson hat on my head and the neckerchief bandanna around my neck were there out of necessity, not for Hollywood to romanticize an era less violent than you would assume. Settlers cared more to live than to strip people of their livelihoods.

I would've stumbled onto the ranch and, before I could head closer, a rifle would sound and soon I'd be history. As I lay dying, I would've heard something like *mighty stupid of you kid, no point risking your life tryin' somethin' like that, we tame our women like we tame our land.* Then Dolkar's husband would've cleaned up the blood, wiped his hands, and thrown me out to the wolves.

Except this wasn't the Wild West.

Except it wasn't as easy as getting shot.

Except I didn't have the time to be *picturing*; I didn't even have the time to breathe.

Half the village came at us with knives and sticks, hollering, "Stop, you bastard!" I took Dolkar's hand in mine, and we were sprinting out of there in screaming colors.

If only it was that simple. The leader of the pack coming after us was her husband. He had the most at stake, makes sense for him to be running the fastest. We ran to the market we met in. Sitting on top of a small hill, this wet market stocked everything from live fish and poultry to fresh fruit, vegetables, herbs, and spices, all on open-air display. Our story isn't what you think it is, and it certainly isn't what it looks like.

Chaos was perfect. The market becomes a hullabaloo on Saturday mornings. Every chance we got, I threw whatever produce I could grab and chucked it at someone. As close to someone as I could in the middle of dodging what currently looks like bok choy to me.

Damn straight, right into his balls. That celery stick made a whole three pointer. *I am Bruce Lee himself.* I mean Michael Jordan. Lebron James. Whatever.

These villagers did not play nice. Two humongous grapefruits hit Dolkar in the ear, knocking her thin body off balance.

"Duck!" I screamed, forgetting that she couldn't understand me. Dolkar got the hint as soon as two more flew over her head.

I stole a box of watermelons from a poor man selling them and rolled them down the road. That bought us some time as I glanced back to see a few of the guys trip. Knocked out like bowling pins. Boom.

"Ay, my watermelon!" The man roared as he jolted awake from his dozing. "Pay me back!" Not that I needed one more person after me, but this one I at least deserved. Needless to say, I probably just rolled days' worth of his income down the street. But our lives were at stake! He will live; we won't. I paid him back in my mind.

Dolkar was falling behind and my arms were exhausted from the watermelons. *Gains, baby!* They were getting closer, wrapping in on us now that the road broke off into a wider one for cars. Except there weren't any. The traffic came from motorcycles, bicycles, or tuk-tuks. We zigzagged through like mice on wheels running through a maze.

A few minutes later, we knelt down next to a buggy to take a breather. The villagers also stopped, looking confused.

Just when it seemed like they'd lost us, I heard, "Behind the yellow shirt!"

Who decided it was a good idea to hide behind a man in a *yellow* shirt? Me, you idiot. They were back on the chase. We kept running toward the red and blue light bars flashing at the end of the street, thinking that was the light at the end of Dolkar's endless tunnel of misery.

I wish I had known it wouldn't be that easy. Nothing was ever that simple.

What does their law say about domestic violence? I read up on it the day before. Prevents it explicitly, of course. Yet, the "law" was zilch compared to what people chose to believe and who they listened to in that village.

As we raced toward the flashing lights, I wish I could tell you I woke up from a restless dream and rolled into school the next day like hooks filmmakers use all the time.

I could not.

if i called Webster would he answer?

―――

"生命的滋味,无论是阳春白雪,青菜豆腐,都要自己去尝一尝啊"

—三毛

Idalia

I was not gorgeous by conventional standards, but I am not being narcissistic when I say my beauty is of the type that transcends time. I could never hold your gaze at first glance, but the longer you looked, the longer you longed to look.

    I had a natural vitality balanced with an elegant bearing—perhaps that's what drew people in. The elegance was a mere demeanor cultivated from education—I made a mess of things, and I laughed at everything; if it really came down to it, it was a face bred by a protective home, and dare I say out loud, a bubble.

As much as I desired to have grown up witnessing more of the world, I couldn't help that when I was in elementary school and wanted earrings, my parents said no.

"But Mom, *you* have ear piercings."

"I'm also thirty-two, and I haven't worn earrings in years."

I resorted to using my measly savings to buy sticker earrings, but that didn't stop me from asking for the real things every year. But every year, the answer was still no. I stopped wanting them in middle school.

I couldn't help it when, in seventh grade, I wanted feathers in my hair like all my white friends, and my immigrant parents were confused.

"Why? What's the point?" my dad asked.

"Umm … there *is* no point. It's pretty," I answered, shrugging.

"Then you don't need it."

"But all my friends have it," I argued.

"Would you also jump off a building if all your friends did?"

"No, I'd be the first." I sulked.

"*Why* would you say that?" He frowned. I didn't know if it was a cultural thing or a my-family thing, but my parents hated it when I brought up death sarcastically, even though they did it themselves. Something about the *way* I phrased it irked them. I didn't get it.

"BASE jumping is a thing, Dad."

He ignored me, turning on the treadmill.

I couldn't help it, when, in eighth grade, I planned to do both track and swimming in high school, but my Asian parents were not amused.

"Do you plan on not studying at all? Or are you close to qualifying for the Olympics?" my dad asked, rhetorically.

"None of the above. I just like both."

"Do you think you're smart or do you plan on not getting into a good college?" my mom questioned, replicating my dad's rhetoric.

I couldn't help it when, toward the end of high school, I wanted to date just for the fun of it, but my Christian parents were horrified. *Illicit affairs?* I had to have grown another head, such was the way they stared at me.

"*For fun?*" they screamed.

"Yeah, I've never been on a date and he's not a bad person—we're both going to different colleges so it's just for fun."

"Listen to yourself. Why would you date without marriage in mind?" my mom interrogated, after she calmed herself.

"Uhh, so I'll know what I want," I stammered, scared she'd start talking about eternal purpose and seeking the Lord and praying for the "right" one right before I left for my casual date. I knew she loved me, that this zeal was the most priceless gift she wanted to influence me with, but I only had the aptitude to think *I need to live* at the time.

"What's the point? Why don't you just go as friends?" she suggested.

"Sure." I headed upstairs to change into jeans. *Friends make out, don't they? Even if it's in jeans?*

I was confident enough to think *Oh I couldn't care less about what I look like. I only want to infiltrate my mind and my soul with more use.* Yet, I knew that if I hadn't been born with beauty that transcended the times, I wouldn't dare to even think like that. Hence, outward appearance was neither a source of pride nor a source of insecurity: I was not too pretty to not be taken seriously, and I didn't think I was too far into the opposite end that I had to waste time being insecure about it.

 I was insecure toward just about everything else, though. My ambition topping all of it—much-too-sweet icing on top of cinnamon apple pie, a taste I hate most in the world. I had *some*, but I never had the brains or gumption or tenacity or talent or discipline or whatever it is you need to follow through with anything. I was always just *okay*: smart enough but not really, hardworking enough but not to where it makes up for not being smart, talented enough but not to where the talent would stick out, friendly enough but not to where it made up for lacking everything else.

 I was perpetually described as *nice* and *respectful*. I hated it. I wanted to call Webster and ask if he'd take those words out of his dictionary, but I'd have to travel back in time. Though scientists proved time travel is theoretically possible, they also said nothing could be changed even if one *were* to go back in time. If it wasn't busy whooping my ass, physics would be remarkable.

 It got to a point where I'd shrink back inwardly every time I heard *nice* or *respectful*. I knew all the "Wow, your daughter's so respectful" and the "Omigosh, thanks! You're so nice" were genuinely compliments, but I wanted to be *more*. I wanted bold, recklessly bold. I wanted independent, fiercely so. I wanted kind, fearlessly kind!

 Unfortunately, those were the type of comments people reserved for those who actually are those things. Nice and respectful were used when there was nothing else to say. If I had a soliloquy, it'd go something like *"when would my life begin?"* or *"can't you see who I really am?"*

 No, they really can't. Unless I show them. Would they care to know?

white flower wilts

그 어느 때보다 빛나는 달이지만 아침이 되어 빛을 잃어가면 어때요.
또 다시 빛날 달인데,
너무 조급해하지 마요.

—ANONYMOUS, NETIZENS

Dolkar

Security never existed for me before Tashi mentioned it. Frankly, I knew the word's denotation, but it never occurred to me that it was an actual possibility. Security. What is that?

My security was slowly watching what little we had get sold off, piece by piece to keep food on the table. My mother's jewelry was all I had left of her and then one day, after school, even the jade earrings disappeared. I searched high and low, near and far, every inch and every valley—though deep down, I already knew the answer.

Two months later, it was the ruby necklace. This one had me heartbroken because this was what I visualized my mother wearing—the only clarity of her misty figure in my mind. I didn't dare approach my father. I didn't dare take the pieces with me for fear the children at school would find out. I started hiding them. From obscure to obvious places, they somehow all disappeared. Nothing of my mother's was left.

Despite the hell she left me in, I still made excuses for her. I wondered if she ever wondered about me. I wondered about her. I wondered what she was like sometimes. It's funny now that I think about it, what I used to think were the worst parts of my life—Father embarrassing himself in front of the entire town after a few drinks, all the children at school making fun of me, taking care of Father, cooking and cleaning for him when no one taught me how—were actually the best parts of my life.

There used to be a little bookshop called Tza-o-Mya in our small town, found in a corner next to the front of our school. After class, I'd hide in the bathroom till everyone was gone, and go straight there. It was one tiny, worn-down shop front, sandwiched between a karaoke place blasting music and a hotpot restaurant rumored to reuse their cooking oil from the gutter. No one noticed this nondescript bookstore, with its sign caked in filth and the advertisements on its windows yellow in age. I wouldn't have noticed it had I not run in there once by accident, hiding from the kids chasing me down.

"Over there! Let's go that way!" I heard one girl scream outside the storefront, as I hid between two tall bookshelves.

"You dumb pig. That street doesn't have anywhere to hide. No way she ran through it that fast," another yelled.

"Let's run down the street with shops," someone suggested.

They gave up ten minutes later, but I have them to thank for giving me everything I loved about life. That day, vellichor wove into my every thought, and I could not walk out of there. The wooden bookshelves towering over me held more books than I'd ever seen in my life. *They must have every book in the world*, I thought, running my hands across the spines. The piles on top looked like they were about to topple over any second.

The owner was always kind. He knew I'd never afford to buy anything, so he let me read as much as I wanted. It quickly became my favorite scene: the smell of yellowed pages infused with time, eras locked into spines, sealed by curious authors once and for all, words that took me to the depths of my imagination. I traveled—around the world and across time, through oceans and over galaxies.

Somewhere in a faraway place, obesity was more common than starvation. And in an ancient land I'd never reach, the most beautiful woman in the kingdom hung herself to death on a pear tree. Along the Rovos Rail on the Pride of Africa, a doctor waited two whole years for her journey.

Inside Tza-o-Mya, I forgot the time, I forgot my name was Dolkar, I forgot everything they said about me: how my mother ran away, how much of a disgrace she was, how my father had been a worthless piece of trash since my mother left, how I was a wild child with no respect. Instead, I became the one sailing the seven seas on a pirate ship, the best-known explorer of the Amazon, the one able to tame even the most ferocious of animals. I became a hero. I read till it was dark, till the owner had to close the shop.

"Next time, sit on the chair over there. The floor's cold," the owner of the bookstore said simply. He was a man of very few words. I nodded gratefully.

Those words were the same words that opened the door to my freedom—I could dream about things beyond where I was. I could be anyone.

Those were the best days.

The sun still rose each day, animals still gathered 'round to play, and I still went to school, but after those boring hours, I was able to learn whatever I felt like learning about. All because of my hidden Tza-o-Mya.

Did you know that octopuses have three hearts?

Did you know that 300 billion atoms make up a drop of water?

That humans are the only animals that blush?

Did you know that pigeons can be trained to tell the difference between a painting by Monet and Picasso?

Before I found my safe haven, my security was hiding in the bathroom every day for lunch and study hall. They said so many things about my mother I didn't know which version to believe anymore. The first time they brought her up was in fifth grade—"daughter of a whore," the girls whispered as I was walking to the bathroom.

"What's a whore?" one boy with big glasses and curly hair asked loudly from the hall behind them.

That was the first time I heard the word as well, but it didn't sound good.

"Nothing you need to know," they snapped at him.

They said she married rich and left. Seeing my dad with his thin, tiny physique, his weathered wrinkles, nervous manner, then seeing me not resemble him at all drove out their wildest imaginations. Well, as wild as their imaginations could stretch.

They said she started her own whorehouse and left the village in shame.

They said she was murdered by drug dealers.

They said a lot about her.

They even said she was a ghost, haunting the promiscuous girls to warn them not to follow in her path.

Gradually, even the classmates who used to be nothing but kind to me started acting cold. At first it was that girl who sneaked me her homework from behind every time I didn't have mine that first stopped giving it to me. Then it was the boy who tore half his eraser apart for me when he realized I didn't have one. Finally it was my best friend—one day she simply said her mom would kill her if she saw her with me again. I was a bad influence. "Because of your bad grades," she had said. I watched her do the things we used to do with someone new.

My security was lying in bed late at night afraid to sleep for fear that *that* fateful night would repeat itself. I was fourteen. Dad ran home, panting. I knew he'd been gambling again; I knew we owed them money. They came knocking every night.

"Pay up." They banged. It sounded no different than dogs growling.

We didn't dare breathe.

"We know you're in there," they repeatedly shouted, until finally they busted through the lock.

"I have nothing left to give," my dad pleaded.

I was peering from behind a door.

They glanced around at our tattered living environment. "He's not lying."

The two men glanced at each other. "You have a daughter."

That's me.

The men looked at each other, they looked at Father, and offered him a time period.

"A year, for all your debt?" they bargained solemnly.

"No, no you can't do that. That's my daughter," my dad pleaded. This was the first time I heard him call me his daughter. This was also the last.

"Then you should've thought twice before going that last round."

"I'm sorry." He looked at his feet. This was the first time I heard him apologize. This was also the last.

"What will it be? Your daughter? Or money?"

"Give me some time. I'll get a job at the factory in the nearest city. I'll send you every penny."

Out of everything spoken, this surprised me most. He could work? Doing what?

I didn't know what "a year" had to do with me. Would I be mopping their floors every day? I could certainly do that, it would be much easier than wood chopping. What if they asked me to chop all their wood for every meal that year? And I'd have to come home only to then do ours? I'd hate it, but it was certainly not impossible.

"Please," they spat out sarcastically. "You've been gambling and drinking since the day your wife left."

"No," my dad screamed, his thin body bristling at them. But he was powerless.

When they walked toward me, I froze in place, knees melting. I didn't think running would've been a solution, and I hadn't the strength to try.

They didn't take the time to advance on me. They simply walked in and grabbed me, like this was normal, the most casual thing people could do.

* * *

pg. 1

neighbor heads to market, apples he brings back;
teacher writes on blackboard, math problem she solves

chicken
ruffles a feather
hen
lays a warm egg
white
flower
wilts
these two men rip my clothes apart
like a wrapper off of a chocolate bar they bought at the
 convenience store
casual
people do this all the time
don't they?

The man with the big belly had ice cold hands.
The other smelled like alcohol; he was gentler but
what even is gentle?
when the very nature of his action ...
they grappled, pushed my knees apart
as much as i tried to hold them together
they slid their hands up my thighs
as much as i shivered
one of them stuck his fingers in there
as confused as i was at what they were doing, i wanted
 them to stop
one of them took off his clothes
i couldn't find my voice

and then they were on me
even if i could find my voice, i wouldn't have been
    able to scream
i closed my eyes
and imagined
it was all a nightmare
why wouldn't it be?
how could it be real?

when it was finally over
when their footsteps had deserted
i found the energy to cry again
cry for my loss ... of what?
i didn't know what they were doing
all i knew, know
is:
i'm not a good girl anymore
i never was considered one
but now?
i'll **never** be a good girl
ever

* * *

That night I cried myself to sleep. I was bleeding, and everything hurt. Dad stood by silently, sober for the first time in what seemed like forever. He didn't know what to do or say, and the unease gave me tension. I shut my eyes and pretended it was a nightmare. When I woke up in the morning, I would go back to being the invisible wall at school no one talks to. I would go back to my worlds of magic and madness in Tza-o-Mya at the corner beside our school owned by the kind old man that opened the doors to all the beauty I've ever experienced in my life.

And soon, very, very soon, I will *get out of here.*

normal suits you not

"Ce qui compte le plus, ce sont les plaisirs simples si abondants que nous pouvons tous en profiter... Le bonheur ne réside pas dans les objets que nous rassemblons autour de nous. Pour le trouver, il suffit d'ouvrir les yeux."

—*LE PETIT PRINCE*, ANTOINE DE SAINT-EXUPÉRY

Idalia

Dude, was this even possible at my age? What started it off were my arguments with my family over the temperature of the AC. I knew I was being unreasonable, but I didn't feel like studying in winter jackets in the dead of summer.

I'd turn the temperature up; Legend would turn it down, back and forth, back and forth. I'd turn it up, Zion would turn it down, repeated a million times.

"Why don't you sit outside?" Legend reasoned.
"Why don't you go downstairs?" I argued.
"I got here first."
"I'm your sister."
"Didn't sign up for this sister." He shrugged, leaving me with the eighty-five degrees. He'd lower it later.

Zion, on the other hand, screamed his head off until I obliged.

"Idalia, I can't do anything when I'm hot," he complained.
"Go downstairs kid!"
"No. You put on a jacket!"
"I did. I'm still cold."
"Put on more. Here, put on mine."
"I can't study if I can't move my arms."
"I can't study when I'm sweating."

He always needed the last word.

I couldn't sleep at night when everything—every joint—hurt because I was cold for no reason. It was not merely a shiver; it was the kind of cold that seeps through your thick dark winter coat, beneath your pores, entangling your muscles, coercing your skeleton to howl with fierce restlessness, jostling your joints loose. When I brought this up to our family doctor, besides the sleeping pills he prescribed with a name I couldn't pronounce, he merely brushed me off, saying I needed more exercise and to put on thicker clothes.

Seriously, doctor? I'm an athlete, thank you very much. Thicker clothes? Did med school charge you a fortune for common sense? Might wanna consider getting a refund.

My parents then sought out a Chinese herbal medicine doctor—he found a multitude of other problems, telling me after one touch of my pulse on my wrist that my body was "off balance." He may as well have stirred up a magic potion and flown home on a broomstick, such was the aura he gave off with his out-of-nowhere diagnosis. He actually did have a cat.

Wonderful, more problems. As if my life isn't one big problem itself.

Off balance was the root of my freezing, freezing when the whole world was burning.

The doctor had ridiculously good handwriting, characters that looked like casual calligraphy without trying, trained by years of waking up at dawn to practice. He reminded me of my grandfather; he also warned me that if I continued swimming outside in the dead of winter like I had to for practice, in a few years' time, I'd approach dangerous infertility.

No, do anything but take away the one thing I care about most.

I couldn't understand, couldn't comprehend—exercise is good, I've always been in top shape, why does this have *anything* to do with infertility? I stared at him in shock, gaping, this was my *life* he was taking away. This was the one thing that made me feel alive after hours of being inadequate at school. They didn't even have a diagnosis for me at the other hospital. Who was this old man sitting in this tiny worn-down clinic telling me I had to choose between my own life and a baby's life? I was eighteen—that was the last thing on my mind.

"Doctor, I can't …," I stuttered, "I don't understand what, what do you mean, why does this have anything to do with …"

His voice was patient and his eyes crinkled in kindness as he explained the concept of balance to me, the foundation of Chinese herbal medicine. "Let's start with something basic: have you ever understood why your mom stresses you to only intake warm drinks or foods on your period?"

"No, I thought she was just being *her*. I thought it was merely old traditions, not backed up by science at all."

"It's not. Your body temperature is around ninety-eight, ninety-nine degrees Fahrenheit normally. Room temperature water is typically around sixty-eight—heat it up a little, and it gets closer to your body temperature. This eliminates disturbance in your body, promoting balance."

"But isn't my body made to balance itself out?"

"You want to make it easier for it or it'll come back to you in other ways, like it's doing precisely this minute."

"Isn't my period coming from my uterus? Why is that connected with the cold in eating or drinking?"

"Your uterus and liver are closely related. Liver maintains vital energy in the body. If any of the channels in the liver, spleen, or kidney are unbalanced, even for a minute, there will be pain. With balance, pain is less likely. Your mother knows best."

"What does this have to do with infertility?"

"Patience, little girl, I'm getting there. Your feet are always cold, it takes hours for you to warm up even in bed with thick blankets. Throughout the day, you can almost count the rare minutes your feet are warm?"

"Yes."

"That means you have a 'cold' uterus—meridians in the feet are connected to your reproductive organs. Imagine trying to hatch an egg without the hen's warmth—it's death, no doubt. That's what will happen to your baby if you keep training the way you do. If you're training in warm water, this doesn't apply. But you told me that they make it freezing cold for competitive reasons—that's detrimental to your uterus because the cold sinks into your body gradually. What'll happen when the time comes is—the embryo has less than a week to implant into the uterus when conception occurs. When implantation happens, the blood vessels, which supply vital nutrients to the developing embryo, are linked with the uterus. This link has to be maintained for at least three months—until the placenta is formed. Your uterus doesn't have the capacity to be weak—one misstep and baby's gone. Which also means you need to cultivate the right environment in these crucial years for when the time comes."

He lost me approximately at word three.

"I got the last part, but you mentioned meridians? I thought that was geography, not body parts."

He laughed his jolly Santa Claus laugh, explaining, "Think of it as your circulatory system to make it simpler. It's the energy distribution system in Chinese Medicine. Instead of thinking of it as a structure, think of it as a process, a flow diagram. You can't pinpoint where it's located—please don't ask how it's developed. You'd have to go to medical school. But this was what we've been using for 5,000 years."

"And you said the meridians in my feet are connected to reproductive organs?"

"Exactly."

"I think ... I understand now."

"You hesitated. Here, here's a broad picture, this is all you need to remember—let's say there's a pool of water, that's your body. You grew up around western medicine. If there's a virus in the pool, western medicine philosophy goes—okay let's kill the virus immediately. That works with cancer or diseases where acting fast is key. In eastern medicine, our philosophy is—how do we cultivate an environment where the virus cannot grow or duplicate? Is it the heat? Is it the cold? What is off balance? We deal with the root of the issue. That's what I'm trying to get you to understand. Eastern medicine takes *time*: weeks, months, years even. It's more of a lifestyle than a cure. Let a few more years go like this and you'll come back to me crying after a miscarriage," he warned sternly, all the jolliness tucked away.

I felt a chill up my spine.

"And remember—even the best Chinese medicine doctors have no cure for patients who don't listen to their lifestyle advice."

And so I quit. My sassy attitude still left me some room to think beyond the present moment. The doctor was right. I wasn't ready to sacrifice fertility for a sport I wasn't even good enough to make a career out of.

I remember sending that last text to my coach to thank him for everything he taught me: I stared at the screen in the dark for hours, heart breaking, deliberating telling him the truth. I typed out the truth and deleted it word by word. I eventually lied, saying my grades were slipping and I had to focus on school. I didn't really know why I lied; maybe I was afraid of his questions. The grades excuse is self-explanatory, but medical problems? What if he asked? What would I say? *Oh, sorry coach, so there's this concept in Chinese medicine called "you can't be too cold." Doctor says I'm too cold, so my nonexistent baby will die.* That sounds like an "I don't feel like going to practice" excuse, somewhere along the same level as "dog ate my homework."

I became even *more* normal—once upon a time I was at least an athlete. Now? Nothing.

Someday ... not then, but someday, I would look back at my relationship with swimming and be completely thankful for our time together. I wouldn't regret a single moment, because throughout middle school, where insecurities flew wild, it was the thing holding together my lifestyle, my pride, and my confidence.

Sometimes, occasionally, I thought ordinary might be best. There is an old Chinese proverb that says "those who tread softly go far." The context? I didn't know. I supposed it had to do with influencing people, approaching situations gently and meekly, taking the high road instead of haggling over little personal gains and losses, but like most Chinese proverbs, it has to do with the grand scheme of life. Tread softly. Don't make a huge commotion, announcing your presence with trumpets and a choir. Even the people who do phenomenal work view themselves as ordinary. Humility. Something like that.

I never wanted to be celebrated; all I wanted was to do something, have a talent, anything that could propel me toward a road of impact. I knew that my sense of justice was too strong for me to live a regular 9-5 till I die, but I was just so normal, so boring it hurt to think about it.

* * *

pg. 7: to all the things I've loved before

Dear things,

I'm sorry I don't have the boldness to chase after you. Swimming was the one long-term relationship. Art? I know, I sucked. You a side hoe. Speaking? I'm not eloquent, nor do I think fast on my feet. You the one I flirted with. Chinese calligraphy? Tried to learn myself, didn't invest in. You're the one who has the crush on me—I just glance your way a few times a year. I'll be crawling back to you once you've already moved on.

Don't hate me,
Idalia

p.s.: if only I could make a career out of becoming a librarian ... nothing's technically stopping me, except everything ... I dream about getting paid to read and travel.

pg. 8: to appease my very terrible case of wanderlust

Grad trip bucket list:

1. Sichuan
2. Gansu
3. Xi'an
4. Chengdu
5. Touristy: Wuzheng, Dunhuang, Pingyao, Fenghuang Gucheng, Wuyuan, Lijiang
6. Trendy cafes: Nbooks Club + more
7. an 'I traveled to another dynasty' photoshoot

Learn about:

1. tea-ism
2. calligraphy

3. chinese painting
4. guzheng / zither
5. chinese poetry
6. chinese herbal medicine

if all plans fail, stay on the road. I'm going back home! and I'm counting down the days. back to the home I never had the privilege to know. save an unprecedented vigor to charm me with, China, because I'm certainly saving mine for you.

he's a turd

Arno

Flash forward: one year and 363 days later.

Along the dirt road, Dolkar and I ran—more like slipped through. Fruit peels, along with bits and pieces of trash, were stuck in the mud. I kicked myself inwardly for not taking the newer road. Decades of "reform and opening up" showed itself most prominently in the roads, I had learned from the village chief two days ago.
Useless if I don't think to use it, I thought, irritated.

We ran and ran and ran and ran: past the little stream where I saw the village kids skip rocks, past the wheat field where I didn't dare to tread for fear of lurking snakes, past the piles and piles of hoggin where transport trucks drove back and forth.

Just when we thought we'd seen wrong, the solid frame of the policeman came into focus. He must've been in the army prior to this job because his back was straight as a rod, despite his head full of white hair. Both Dolkar and I—well, Dolkar explained while I mimed—tried to tell him they were coming after *us*, we were the ones *escaping*, but I guess there were holes in our story because he told us to shut up and get in his car.

"Please," Dolkar pleaded with all the life she had left, "let me *go*."

"Get in the car," he said, sentencing her life away as simply as that.

"Sir, if you have any decency left …" she panted.

He didn't let her finish before shoving her in his car.

The drive was short, but hot. I couldn't tell you what went on outside because I was busy drowning in my sweat. After maybe three minutes, we pulled up to the station. It was a little eerie—illuminated in dark, yellow-ish light, like some old worn-down Procter & Gamble factory. As we walked into the station, the only thing that didn't match the setting was the noise—four officers at each table, they slapped down cards, shouting things I didn't understand as they spat out sunflower seeds. They had time for this? Hell, have they always been this oblivious to what's going on inside a home five minutes away from there?

Once inside the room, they didn't need to keep me isolated to get me to start talking.

"Whatever he's about to say, he is a pathological liar!" I shouted into Google Translate as I glared Dolkar's husband down, Google's robotic voice drowning out all my fury. I wish I could light that robot on fire. Unable to get my point across, my fury boiled into my brain, blocking out what might've been some neurological pathways. I knew they weren't getting it because these *criminals* were still laughing. At me.

"Liar? That's all you got?" Google translated from his phone, as Dolkar's husband crackled. This whole situation would almost be comedic if so much wasn't at stake.

I couldn't believe what I was hearing. I almost wish expressions could be lost in translation, but some expressions happen to be universal. The sneer he wore from the second he walked in practically knocked me off my chair. That ugly looking face of his—I wanted to punch his nose off. His lack of heart. His lack of emotion. His lack of anything humane. Had I just met a sociopath? What the hell. I thought sociopaths were pretty intelligent. *This* guy? He was a turd. A waste of space. I stared at that nasty looking face—those two gigantic moles by his nose looked like owl eyes. *If he looks at me with that sneer of his one more time, I'll knock those owl eyes out.*

I turned back toward the officer, handing him what I'd typed on my phone: *I am only a friend. Her husband is killing her.*

He didn't seem surprised. I would've investigated into the actual criminal had the case been mine. *This guy literally has one job. Probably been sucking on sunflower seeds all day to know how to do it, though.* If I had been his boss, I'd rather hire a grilled cheese sandwich than him.

He shook his head and eyed us with a look of pity—*well he is her registered husband.*

Pity! Pity solves nothing—*get this girl out of his hands dammit!*

Her husband's sneer continued to hang on his hideous face.

I couldn't take this anymore—I lunged.

Right there, in front of the entire police station. *Shoot me now.*

festering sore

> "For a transitory enchanted moment man must have held his breath in the presence of this continent, compelled into an aesthetic contemplation he neither understood nor desired, face to face for the last time in history with something commensurate to his capacity for wonder..."
>
> —THE GREAT GATSBY, F. SCOTT FITZGERALD

Idalia

My favorite place in the world is on a plane—if I can, I always try booking a time when I'd see the sunrise. When every cloud outside my window is basked in its light, as if the sky itself could speak of love—what a marvel that is to behold. This is when I'd escalate my wonder: what adventures await me when I land?

What if I get bit by a lizard and turn into a dragon?

What would happen if I get recruited to drink an experimental serum and wake up in the twenty-second century to an internationalist world with no borders?

These are the types of thoughts that run through my mind on the plane after my movie marathons. As crazy as I was about *Captain America*, Marvel didn't do much to influence my thoughts. They were of my very own. Obviously.

I intentionally stayed up all night watching movies right before my trip so I could fall asleep on the plane. That way, as soon as I landed, *voilà*, I wouldn't waste time dealing with jet lag; I needed every minute to travel! What I didn't account for was the chance that I wouldn't be able to fall asleep despite staying up all night.

My sleep deprivation was actually ridiculous. People suffer from insomnia for palpable things like trauma or death or sickness or finances. Not me—I couldn't sleep because I kept thinking *I'm too "plain."* Whatever that means. I thought this trip was supposed to get me to step out of the wallow of anger I'd sunk myself in to, not intensify it. I know I'm lucky—incredibly lucky to be where I was: no tumultuous upbringing, enough opportunity to chase after what I wanted (if I could figure out what I really want), not too much privilege to where I had to live in the shadow of my family's accomplishments, no special talent, nothing worth mentioning. Normal. Loving family. Stable.

But—wicked irony—that's our problem here, isn't it?

I tried to remember how lucky I was to have only known a life filled more with certainty than uncertainty ... because as I was sitting there, mooning over possibilities of something different, someone else would kill just for a little taste of security.

Shut up, me, I told myself. *You're so annoying, go to sleep already.*

I didn't like counting sheep, so instead, I counted stars. *One, two, three* ... Eight hundred fifty-five stars later, I was still wide awake.

My life was literally proof that I didn't need a drug problem or a toxic relationship or anything at all for me to ruin it; I had a perfectly fine blueprint before I started living it. What the Hades.

I sat up to ask for water, hesitating for a second to plaster a polite smile on my face before I pressed the button. I did not feel like smiling. It did not matter.

Attractiveness one thousand percent plays into whether flight attendants on Air China get hired, I thought as the woman came by. Asians love a picturesque "no-makeup" makeup look—this woman had nailed it down to an artform.

"Is there anything else I can get you?" she asked sweetly, after handing me the water I requested.

"No thank you," I answered sweetly, mirroring her tone.

I got in trouble all the time when I was younger for not having a façade, for displaying my face like an open book. One time I woke up, excited for my first violin class, only to discover my parents had to cancel on me because we had a guest. I clunked the water I was supposed to bring him with a loud *bang* on the coffee table, and the thought of violin class became history. My parents were furious. I was roughly pulled aside to another room; I would've gotten more than that telling-off had the guest not been there. Should I have been thankful? Probably. Was I? No. Every emotion was written plainly on my face.

"What was that for?" My dad lectured as loud as he could without the guest being able to hear.

"What? I'm mad, I ..." I sulked.

"With no right to be. I'm not raising a little brat in this house," my dad interjected.

FESTERING SORE · 55

"I'm just being real. I'm mad, and I'd act mad even if I was alone and he wasn't here."

"*Real* does not give you an excuse to be rude."

"So? I'd rather be real and rude than fake and polite," I defended myself.

"Nonsense. There's no reason you can't be polite and real."

"I can't."

"Then make yourself."

"I don't want to be fake. I want to be real." I pouted.

"Idalia, seriously. This discussion is unnecessary. Go out there, put on your brightest smile, and bring out the tea *gently*. Or I'll guarantee you'll never see a violin in your life."

"No. Make me. I don't wanna learn anyways."

"Regardless, you *will* drop that attitude," he warned.

"No."

"No what? Why?"

"*You're* making me mad now."

"We'll talk about this later. If you think polite is fake, be fake right now."

"That's absurd. I can't be myself?"

"I don't care what you think. Do as I say. Remember—anyone who thinks they're being themselves by displaying what they feel plainly on their face, like you're doing, is someone who can't control their emotions."

"I *can* control it—I just don't *want* to."

"End of discussion."

I wish it really was "end of discussion." Except various versions of this conversation occurred multiple times over the years, all along the lines of pointing out how low of an EQ I had.

Sleep, where are you? The longer I stayed awake the more jet lagged I'd be.

I started over, this time squaring horses. *Four, sixteen, two hundred fifty-six ...*
I counted up all two hundred fifty six horses of all shades and shapes, and still not a wink of sleep.

I wanted to fly off to Tibet or Mongolia; I wanted to explore the un-touristy places. Alas, what would my relatives think if I didn't visit them first? I had to, am obliged to, no reason not to go around visiting relatives first. I'm not *free.*

Free. What does that mean?

In every situation where I had a "my heart" versus "what everyone expects" dilemma, I tried to keep in mind that duty and responsibility always goes before freedom.

Is it really supposed to?

I knew that freedom was not about doing what you want when you want—it's about having the choice between different roads, all of them difficult, all of them with different risks and rewards, but ultimately having the choice in your hands. If there was no duty nor sacrifice, there would be no freedom to speak of. The very existence of freedom calls either sacrifice or duty into action.

But how free can I really be when duty and responsibility are taking up so much room? Which begs the question: what if I prioritized doing whatever I want when I want? So long as it doesn't negatively affect anyone else. Then would I be free?

I'd thought long and hard about the concept of freedom through sleepless nights, hearing the clock tick by second after second for hours at a time. The insomnia wasn't too bad on the rare days I finished my work, but on the days where all I did was watch Shawn Mendes or Jackie Chan interviews, wasting away my time but unable to muster up the productivity level to do something, with curfew at midnight at my house, I'd lay awake all night thinking: *This is why I don't have my aspirations work out—any of them. This is why I can't have nice things.*

Then I'd come home the next day—dead tired, lacking sleep, and unable to focus again; I'd watch one episode of some show while repeating "last one" after every episode, and start the toxic cycle all over again the next day. The toxicity forced me to wonder, ponder, deliberate, debate, scream, shout, break down, cry about whether I had it all wrong, everything: what if I *could* do something out of the things I love? Those things, I never struggled learning about or finishing assignments for. I'd never been the one that was good at everything or so good at something it seemed worth throwing away other things for. I didn't think I had the tenacity to "make it" when I didn't know exactly what I was supposed to "make it" in. Without that confidence or grounded-ness, I'd stumble into this model minority trap. It was always the math and science that killed me inside. Because I was *supposed* to be good at it but was not.

What if I could be free to *write*, let's say? Or study enough literature to keep in my arsenal to write in the future? Or languages? I had a knack for languages. Language is *the key* to culture! Without language, we would only be half alive.

What if? What if? What if?

Sleep eventually found me when it saw the number of *what if*s welling up my mind.

my daughter, go make something of yourself

Dolkar

Monsoon season was close; I felt it in the breeze, wisps of cooler air amidst the weeks of endless heat. In the darkness, plastic underneath me shuffled as I churned around and around. There were seconds in the night I let myself linger over the only luxury I could afford: imagining the idea of possibilities.

The whole village knew Naing had parents who both worked in a factory in the city; she gave the stray dogs bones and loaned the girls at school her bright pink nail polish.

Myat had two brothers who each plowed the fields behind their oxen every season; he climbed up the mountain to the monastery to burn incense for the gods—when he prayed, they listened.

Thein had an uncle who bought a house in the city and married the daughter of a merchant; every year he came back with shiny new clothes. Every year, another young boy was seen wearing something he outgrew.

In my culture, we greeted each other with *mingalaba*, a blessing of sorts. "Mingalaba," I'd say each morning, bowing to my teacher. "Mingalaba," I'd say as I passed by the women swinging their hoes in unison, chanting *one, two, one, two* with each swing. "Mingalaba," I'd say to the monk who occasionally came down the mountain; when he nodded, I got a feeling I might really be blessed that day.

Tonight, I ripped a strand of my hair out each time *mingalaba* entered my mind; it was the word they used right before they picked me up and threw me on the floor.

I woke up with the rooster's call as per usual. For a while I didn't think I could make it out of bed. My stomach hurt; I felt nauseous, like any movement beyond laying there would spill out my intestines. Last night came flashing back to me in torn up fragments. *No, I can't think about it. It didn't happen; I imagined all of it. I don't have the luxury to mourn over last night. The more I do, the less I'll feel.* So I dragged myself out of bed, nearly crawling on all fours.

Nothing but a normal day.

I sat down near the stone slab, ready to make a cooling paste to protect my skin from the sun. I poured a single drop of water on it and rubbed thanaka bark round and round the stone slab until the motion reminded me ...

Ahhhh! Ah ahhhhhhh!

I threw the bark across the room, toppling a cup with a loud *bang*. We couldn't afford to break that cup; I didn't think about it. I ran outside, letting out the long shrill I'd held in all night. *Why me? Why why why why why why why*

why why? I gave thanks when I wanted to kill. I smiled when I wanted to cry. Why why why is it always me?

That village never needed to worry about another dry season: I cried out my weight. When I'd finally exhausted myself, I got up like it was nothing but a normal day.

Nothing but a normal day, I echoed.

I fed chickens and pigs. I watered what little was left of our garden.

As I was packing my backpack for school, I realized Dad wasn't there. Last time he was up that early might've been when he didn't go to sleep.

As I was contemplating where he could be or what he was doing, he walked inside the house with a bag of groceries. Shocking.

He simply said, "Dolkar, give me your backpack."

I handed it to him. He emptied out my books, wordlessly and aggressively dumping all the contents onto the table. He whirled around the house like a hurricane swirling things into my backpack. After ten minutes, he handed it to me.

"You need to leave," Dad rushed the words out, unable to look me in the eye.

It took me a minute to register. I blinked twice, "Leave? To where?"

I could tell it was hard for him to say this, but eventually he was able to utter: "You're not safe here. Mr. Han knows someone he met when he was in China. He called that man, and he agreed to send someone to pick you up as soon as you're off the train. You'll work for his family at their homestay."

"Why? I—"

He interjected quickly. "Those men will come back. They will keep doing it to you. I don't know how to protect you."

"What about you?" I asked carefully.

"I am the last thing you need to worry about. Go. Go work for him. Any wage is better than this hellhole."

He handed me a train ticket to the nearest city along with a stack of cash, by all means the most I'd ever seen in my life; I think it was definitely the rest of what he had, all he ever had. I don't think he left anything for himself. *How will he live?*

"Go now," he repeated, "before they come back."

I took the backpack and the bag of food in my hands. We treaded out toward the nearest train station.

"What if they ask where I went?" I posed the question quietly.

"I'll tell them you couldn't take the shame, so you ran away."

"What if they threaten to do things to you?" I dug further.

"I have nothing else they'd want," he replied stoically.

"What if they torture you for the money?" I panted, slightly jogging to catch up to his pace.

"I've known them for years. They only go that far if there's something they want: money or sex. Organized crime, they're not stupid."

I stopped my questioning for the rest of the walk.

The train station was packed. It smelled weird, a jumble of different scents I couldn't pinpoint. It was my first time riding a train, and it would've been exciting had the situation not been as dire, had I not felt that tired or sore all over. I'd never seen so many humans in one place. I'd never seen that many people, period.

Dad seemed lost and overwhelmed as well, caught in the middle of a sea of people. He frantically looked behind himself several times to make sure I was following. I savored his concern, knowing soon it would be gone. He was always drunk, always somewhere else, but even in his darkest moments, he never laid a finger on me. I guess that was his love for me. I guess that was all I could ask for.

Since we got there a bit early, we had enough time to find our way to the right place. I made my way up the train and found my seat. Then it was time to go.

"Take care of yourself!" he screamed, slamming hard on the glass outside.

I kept nodding, but my voice was constricted in my throat. The train started driving, and I could see him running to catch up to it. My last image of him burned out all those years of neglect. His thin frame doubled over, panting, his eyes red. He looked a decade older than his actual age. And suddenly I understood: I looked too much like Mom for him to face me. Oh, *oh*.

It wasn't until a few hours in that I realized he never once mentioned seeing me again.

a mea culpa

Idalia

pg. 9: Metaphors Maybes and Mutterings

let them go then, Madeline
before the light sucks up to the night
again
let us go, through tentative one-night plans,
the snarling void
of quiet whisperings of doubt
let us go, through restless minds,
the growling vacuum
of demanding voices to be done about
let us go, through long drives with windows down
the howling wind
of a deep dark town
let us go
till we never stop going—

voices
the ones that surround like a mythical creature
it frowned
beats the secret
the one that holds the key to life and death
out of the hero
oh Lady Macbeth
and the creature is just <u>one</u> out of the many
    in the labyrinth
and the voice is just <u>one</u> out of the only in
    my mind

into the board room they all go
talking of Cristiano Ronaldo

oh we have lingered too long
on songs filled with plans
on demands filled too strong
excuses
too long
sharp knife trembling in her hands
last she stands
foam
arise

into the board room of their clients
betting on the New York Giants

oh, we've been lingering too long
the Lençóis Maranhense of Brazil
highlands of Iceland
glaciers of Patagonia would subdue

*so long as it quiets the drizzling
riots, riots*

*do not
ask what
only
ask when*

* * *

Asia never seems to run out of ideas for its cafes. I'd heard Asia being described as the ideal mood board for dining and beverage industries. It seeks new, it seeks fast, and its cuisine is inherently diverse. Tea culture is strong, and the influx of coffee is prevalent.

Every few steps was a new design, a popping dose of innovative advertisement striking my senses. I'd walked past the chance to earn a suitcase, coupons that could (yeah right) earn me a ticket to some concert of a celebrity I did not care about, a free hour of karaoke, and an insane amount of free taste tests. When the window of a café displayed a bookshelf of brown, faded leather-bound notebooks with notes left by customers, I could no longer move my feet. That's how I found myself sitting on a funky red sofa with my own faded leather notebook, an Americano, and a flyer that read "afraid to try something new?" in my hands.

Challenge accepted. I had walked in defiantly and ordered a flavor of ice cream called "Spicy—Do Not Try. Get Something Else."

I did not get something else.

"Are you sure?" the green contact-wearing cashier confirmed with me. Again. For the eightieth time.

I held up the flyer. "Of course."

I immediately regretted ordering that disgusting flavor of ice cream. Who in the galaxy decided it was a good idea? Oh that's right, marketing directors who had clearly done research into my brain. It's like they were targeting idiots like me. Because I ordered something else right after to get rid of the taste.

Flipping through a worn notebook on the shelf behind me, I couldn't help noticing an entry someone left:

I want to make you proud, but what do I do now?
When my dreams don't align with yours for me?
What now?

I took a moment to reflect. I'd never forget that argument, the biggest one I'd ever had with my parents. It started with a major disagreement that increasingly blew up until things were shattering across the room and our neighbors called the police.

"I'm in love with culture, you can't take that away from me," I remember arguing.

"What will you do with a liberal arts degree? Lobby for human rights?" my dad challenged.

"I don't know. All I know is I love languages."

"Do that in your free time, or after you're financially independent. At that point, you can draw butterflies for a living for all I care. But right now, with my money, I need you to able to define your career path, calculate out the investments versus your returns, and identify a broader range of choices than what I foresee with linguistics." He frowned at the last word.

"I don't need a broad range when I already know what I want! I can make money with it! I'll show you! Google Translate hires linguistics majors. Apple too; Siri needs to be developed."

"Do you like computer science? If you combined that with linguistics, then go ahead and do it," my mom suggested.

"No. I hate computer science."

"Then for the love of God do not bring it up again. It's like you live in Disney World or something. Apple and Google are two of the most competitive companies in the world. Google only has a certain number of people working on Google Translate—name one reason they wouldn't hire linguistics majors from Harvard or Yale. Name one of your selling points against Harvard grads," my dad continued.

I later realized that I had started to lose all reason at some point. All I saw were my dreams, visions, hopes, and plans holding their hands out to me to save them from drowning with the tide. My parents continued convincing me that if I didn't have choices by graduation—that if I was desolate and starving—I wouldn't have the capacity to be creative and do what I love.

"But ... but I love languages more than I love life itself. It builds bridges, connects cultures, connects people! Isn't that the meaning of life? Or at least the meaning of my life. I'd very willingly give my life's worth of work to something as beautiful and as sacred as languages, connection, and culture," I expressed.

Between the two of them, they kept splashing buckets of cold water on me. Not literally. I, however, am a stubborn person. I continued.

"But ... Jackie Kennedy got her Bachelor's in French Literature! And when she toured France, President Kennedy described himself as the 'man who accompanied Mrs. Kennedy to Paris.' And he said that in the sixties! Isn't that powerful? Isn't that fascinating? There's so much I could do with linguistics!"

"Maybe use your Jackie example after you get a 'Kennedy' in your name, shall we?" remarked my mom.

My dreams were so far near the edge of the waterfall I could hear myself telling them to go to someone more willing to fight. I lost more reason. My arguments didn't even make sense anymore.

"What? Are you also about to tell me that a husband is a greater asset than a degree too?" I demanded.

All three of us already made our points, and any more words would've been unnecessary thirty rounds ago. But things didn't stop there.

"Forget your gallant pride and suck up to society!" my dad shouted, having finally lost his patience with me.

Things escalated; reason was so beyond lost that it fell off the map; I knocked over a vase; my dad knocked over a plant. The police came and asked what we were up to.

"Nothing," all three of us snapped. The officer raised an eyebrow.

"Is there any way I can help?" he asked politely.

"Not unless you have a way to hook me up with a Kennedy." I scowled, rolling my eyes. My smiling façade got lost too, somewhere in the midst of losing reason. "Idalia!" Both my parents were shocked I'd said that. They were used to succumbing to authority, no matter the request. That's why they sacrificed their entire lives to give me choices. And to them, I was choosing wrong.

*I want to make you proud, but what do I do now?
When my dreams don't align with yours for me?
What now?*

he just looks like a waste of space

Arno

Flash forward: one year and 354 days later.

I couldn't tell you whether they dropped their cards in shock or widened their eyes or whatever it is police do when they see someone tackle the criminal in their own territory. The criminal they won't lock up. All I knew was that I saw red; all I knew was that I was riding on top of him, hurling punches faster than you could say stop; all I knew was I wanted the red I saw manifested on his face. With rhythm. Weak idiot couldn't even fight back.

Bam. "Don't you dare touch her again!"
Thwack. "You son of a ..."
Wham.

I felt someone pull me off of him. Dolkar's husband squinted up at me from the ground—looking even more like a waste of space. We don't have enough space on earth for landfill, much less him.

Dolkar stood there watching me as two officers pressed me down into a chair; another officer ran into the room next door—I couldn't decipher what the look on her face meant. Calm? Disgust? Awe? Indifference? Thankfulness?

Are you okay? I gestured. She nodded slowly, then pointed at me.

Me? I questioned, pointing at myself. *Do I look that bad?* I gave her a thumbs up, grinning. *He was easy, you kidding?*

I'm guessing the brief shake of her head meant she didn't seem convinced. In response, I cupped my hands and raised it like a toast. *First day, first adventure. We're kicking this off at the police station. Here's to the next few days.*

I could have been walking out of the station had I not continued to stick my nose in Dolkar's business, but instead, I was directed to an office down the hall for "further questioning." A skinny looking nerd sat at a big wooden desk with his feet propped up. His face was blank, like he forgot what emotions were a decade ago when his mother died. Something like that. I hope she didn't actually die.

"I'm Officer Suo." He gestured at the plastic chair in front of his desk.

"And I'm fucked!" I plopped down.

Both introductions were lost in translation. He looked more like he belonged in front of Java or Python than on the streets arresting someone. Or even inside a police station questioning someone. Messy, greasy, spiky hair and a haircut that looked like his blind grandma did it. Thick Harry Potter glasses. Drinking from a hot water bottle with Pikachu on the lid.

"Explain," he ordered. No further words, only those four syllables that translated into one command.

I gave him my phone, opened up to Google Translate: *I am only a friend of the girl outside. Her husband is killing her.*

He looked at me in confusion, as if saying: how is that your business?

I wanted to answer, *Well if you did your job right, I wouldn't have to be the one doing it*, but what he said next prevented me from saying anything at all.

Instead of interrogating me on why I thought that was my business, he asked, "How did you know?"

i need more time

"天生我材必有用,千金散尽还复来"

—李白·《将进酒》

Idalia

"Because men are more important than women," my great aunt concluded firmly, her tone matter of fact.

No, she wasn't whispering. No, it wasn't a joke. No, she wasn't quoting anyone.

She was dead serious.

I wanted to hit something, but I kept walking, as if she was right. I wanted to shout at someone, but I said nothing, at least not in front of the dead. I wanted to tell her she was outrageously wrong, but if I did, it would be "disrespectful."

In that moment, it took every bit of class I'd cultivated since birth to respect my own culture: we do not talk back forcibly to our elders.

So instead, I shed silent tears. I somehow managed to control my actions and my words, but no one could control my gushing stream of thoughts.

Calm down. This insignificant place is not your battleground.

I wiped my tears away, and tried to breathe—in through my nose, out through my mouth.

She's old and uneducated. It's not her—it's the environment of the province she grew up in. Breathe.

I could not fathom the idea of such a world; how did they view their mothers? My mom was always my hero. She never taught me to view her as such—I simply did because she took care of everything, and always with grace. Moreover, how did women in such a world view themselves? As subservient to men? For *what?*

I thought back to the past few days. Every little detail I was uncomfortable with—they somehow all snowballed together into an effect that was a tenth of a millimeter away from me spewing out fire.

The entire time we were in Henan, I had my sweetest smile tacked on; I asked my relatives questions; I was genuinely interested in how they were doing; I initiated conversation. Zion was playing Fortnite; Legend slumped back in his chair in a glazed-over look, disinterested. At the family dinner, as I walked over to sit in the one chair left by my great uncle, he smiled at Legend, called him over to be the one sitting next to him.

"Legend—Uncle's specifically calling for you." My dad laughed, pridefully oblivious. The rural community had mocked him when I was born.

I didn't say anything.

As I sat down next to my great aunt, I thought of finding out more about my grandfather, since I didn't remember meeting him, and my dad never told us much. All I knew was how stringent he was with his sons, and that he'd multiply that discipline toward himself two-fold. If he required them to wake up at seven to study, he himself would be up by five to practice calligraphy.

"What was my grandfather like?" I asked my great aunt.

"Ahh ... your grandfather," she reminisced. "Responsible. He took it upon himself to take care of everything so we could all eat."

I discovered that his calligraphy was known throughout the region—before the cultural revolution, that is. Businessmen sought him out to brand their storefront signs; government officials received his art pieces as gifts; everyone else he politely turned away. I wanted more than anything for him to have been able to teach me, but I wasn't allotted the time to discover what he was like.

Alas, such is the price you pay when your parents are foreigners on someone else's land. You could have the most intriguing family in the world, but without proximity, you wouldn't get to know them as people until you visited. You struggle to make a foreign home your own. You struggle to make your parents' former home your own. You struggle with who they are. You struggle with who you are.

Everything would've ended on a bittersweet note had I not opened up another can of worms. "What about my grandmother? When did they meet?"

My great aunt never answered my question. She went on to imply that with my grandfather's education, he was always out of my grandmother's league, and blatantly stated that he married her to fulfill his filial piety when their mother was sick. "Because your grandmother was from the rural area, she knew how to take care of people; she was diligent," she had commented, almost as if it were a compliment that my grandmother got to marry into their family.

I could not believe the nerve—my grandmother was one of the most tenacious people I knew. Who gave this aunt the right to say something like that?

I could still remember my grandmother's visits to America. In more carefree days, I thought the biggest problem I'd ever encounter was my parents' rage. Dad had assigned a long poem for me to memorize—the longest one I'd ever seen. It was Li Bai, but while his poetry I'd seen before was only four lines, this one had twelve! I was devastated. I ran around the neighborhood playing all afternoon, only to remember I had to memorize that poem when dusk fell.

I sprinted home. "Grandma! Grandma, what do I do?"

"Sit down and memorize it," she replied calmly, peeling potatoes for dinner.

"He's your son! Do something, please!"

My grandma got up to chop her potatoes. "I can't do anything if I agree with him—that's a really good poem for you to memorize."

"I can't finish this stupid poem! This is jail!" I cried.

"You know, I heard if you eat your book it'll get in your brain faster."

My eyes grew wide with excitement. Before she could look my way, I tore off that page of my poetry textbook and had it in my mouth.

She stormed over, vaguely shocked. "I was kidding!"

While I did get in trouble that night, everything was okay as long as my grandma was there to wipe away my tears.

And now here was this woman I'd never met, implying awful things about her; I didn't know how to retort.

I stopped my questioning, disgusted, but not before smiling stiffly and nodding, all while hating myself for not saying anything for my grandmother.

At the grave site, we performed a ritual where we burned paper and blasted firecrackers to honor the dead. The paper was believed to be money that the dead could use in their next life, and the firecrackers were meant to awaken them so they could come get the money. Even as a Christian, I did my part at each grave we went to. In my heart, I asked for forgiveness, all while viewing it more as culture than as religion. As I stepped forward to burn my part of the paper at the last grave site, I was told Legend, Zion, and my dad needed to go before my mother and me.

"Why?" I questioned, the first time I'd stepped out of line our entire trip.

No one answered. It was obvious; we were feebleminded, clearly the weaker, incompetent portion of the population. The sex that deserved to be killed if parents could only have one child. The sex that deserved to be killed if resources were scarce. The sex whose one vocation on earth was to lift the other sex up.

"*Because men are more important than women.*"

I held it all in until I couldn't anymore. Back at the hotel, I screamed at my dad for not backing me up. Alone and in front of my parents, there *was* no grace nor class; I dropped the act and unleashed it all.

"You would stand there and let them verbally abuse me like that? This is your family; it's not my place to say anything—you taught me that! The generational gap is too wide, that I'm not allowed to talk back to my elders. I was crying for you to say something! And what did you do? You *stood* there."

My dad patiently echoed the thoughts I was afraid to admit. "Did you want me to scream at her? Lecture her? *My* elder? What good could I do? We're leaving tomorrow morning; better to end things on a good note. We're only here every few years. She has believed in sexism her whole life, even if it meant undermining *herself*. Get over it. Prove them wrong. Accomplish something great."

What did I have to accomplish to bring honor to my family? Being a CEO? Doctor? Lawyer? Going to Harvard, Yale, Princeton? Next stop President?

"Look, right there! That's modern sexism. I have to *prove* them wrong? While Legend and Zion sit there and are already accepted for who they are?"

Technically, I was wrong about Legend and Zion; they could not just sit there, but my dad let me scream my head off without responding. He listened to my tirade.

"Has she been living under a rock? Let me tell you about the women I see in this generation, women who had it in them to always be like this generation, but were stigmatized for trying anything different. They are strong, intelligent, independent, resilient, beautiful, tenacious, passionate, incredible women. *People*. Whatever they identify as. We have people who are working tirelessly trying to become not just kind or just honest or just compassionate but every one of those traits and more, who find the energy to sacrifice for their families while working vigorously toward their dreams, who love beautifully and walk gracefully."

"I agree," my dad expressed softly.

I was still not done, though in hindsight I wish I could take back the words I said next.

"Mom's family, old to young, treats every *person* equally. I'd rather be with them."

That did it.

My dad erupted. "Idalia! I'm ashamed of you—be ashamed of yourself. Have you no decency? They have been taking us all over the place since we got here: dinners, tourist spots, hotels. They're seventy, eighty years old! What else do you expect from them? Have some grace, my God! You think it was fair for me growing up? For them? Life! Is never fair. Get used to it. You won't see the justice you want to fight for, for as long as you live."

Dad was the second child, the extra. The one without a birthright. My temper tantrum was immature. Someday when my grace and class was cultivated to the amount of control I had before arriving at this hotel, I'd be a great woman. I always hurt the people who love me most; I always get hurt most by the people I love.

I would go on to learn that we *must not judge people by our standards but by the standards that existed at their time.* Just as I viewed equality as the unshakable standard, they grew up in a society where sexism was the bedrock. Boys brought in income; they left the legacy, brought honor to their families, passed down the family name. Equality: my norm. Sexism: their norm. It devastated me, but I was one girl against a generation of people who grew up being taught that was the case. To fight inequality, we'd need everyone on board. There *are* brave *men* out there, outspoken feminists, fighting for a future alongside their daughters and sisters and mothers and wives. It's a human fight. Just like with race. Or class.

And just like with race or class, all the -isms we label ideas with—sexism, racism, ageism—we shouldn't throw around lightly because doing so would taint the blatant crime of the action or thought itself. No one *is* sexist. No one *is* racist— because it's not a fundamental identity. People can change.

I would also come to realize that, because of family bonds and bloodlines that go beyond my recognition, beyond *myself*, I am a plethora of stories worth telling about.

I am a series of paradoxes worth exploring and, no matter where I go, I *will* carve out a path of legacy worth reading about.

* * *

pg. 12

tear-stained, my great aunt waved us goodbye
holding my hand, my great uncle almost pleaded, "come visit soon"
I heard the words he didn't say: "before it's too late"

I will, I will go back soon

and all at once, all the fury evaporated, and all I had left was heartbreak
maybe proximity would allow them to see me
as a person
not a category

maybe my judgment had been too harsh

I wish
I had more time with them, too

* * *

Things were a lot less dramatic with my mom's family. At home in America, with the distance, I was used to my grandfather's absence. But this time, at his own house, with him not there, his absence blared at me from all the memories of him in my mind.

All the fun we had together.

I was young; it had been raining all day. I longed to be outside, climbing trees and jumping fences. I'd been practically bouncing off the walls since daybreak, with nothing to do. Bored out of my mind, I tried to draw and got frustrated. He picked up my color pencils and showed me how to use simple shapes to form masterpieces. My flower was a circle surrounded by some triangles and a line. But he told me he'd never seen one more beautiful in his life.

I complained he was lying to me, that I still wanted to go climb a tree.

He promised to race me upstairs! We went up and down ten thousand times; I won every time.

"You're *this* close to making the Olympics." He spread his index finger and thumb a centimeter apart.

He was sixty-five, and he had all the energy in the universe for me; being worlds apart, I didn't even make it to his funeral. Not only that, months before he died, I had been too scared to sit next to him. I'll be sorry for the rest of my life.

My grandma still lived there, and there will never be a day when I don't look up to her.

The simple moments with her were the best. I was having coffee with eggs, bacon, and toast. She was having porridge with sweet potatoes, vegetables, and a hard-boiled egg. Her Bible was open, bright purple reading glasses on, asking me characters she was never taught as she struggled to learn to read by herself. Character by character, word by word, she traced the sentences bit by bit in her wrinkled, weathered hands. Hands that had reaped the harvests of good years and buried the life of a son.

    I stared at her in amazement, the same way I always did. This was a woman who, being the oldest, was deprived of an education; this was a woman who worked in the fields to provide for her family. At eighty, she finally had time to rest. But what was she doing instead? Teaching herself to read. Her self-control was immeasurable, one that I could only dream about possessing.

    I didn't know how to tell my grandma I admired her. A phoenix out of the ashes. I'd always see that in her.

* * *

pg. 13

I am only allotted the time to fiercely love a limited number of people in my lifetime. I'd greedily want to include more people, but alas, my regret weighs on me heavier than anything I can do to shake it off.

I need
more
time;

they gave it all
so their children could Be more

did they stop to look back
at everything they lost?

he had his cold, wicked pride
an iron-clad work ethic

she had this spicy, radiant warmth
a fierce love for everyone she touched

and they were unstoppable

heading toward a world they did not know or
understand, a world waving a flag they thought
would cure their lust for freedom

standing face-to-face with
language barriers
loneliness
a global recession

and even still

they remained unstoppable

i'm a frog

Dolkar

Receding rapidly behind me were the sights of never-ending rice fields. More villages. More plains. Cottages thatched by palm leaves. I lost count of how many. Twilight, faint and fragile and light, breathed calmly now, unleashing soft wisps of fury gathered by the devilish sun at noon. The train continued clickety-clacking past each village. Children waved enthusiastically, and the couple in front of me waved back, smiling. They were shades I had never seen on people before, a pale white I had only read about in history books. Something about their empire being so vast the sun never sets on it. Or was it something else about standing up against Communism in a Cold War? I did not know which was which.

As the train slowed to a crawl, I followed my father's exact directions. I got off the train. I went directly outside of the station, spotting the gray car with a sign on the window saying Dolkar. Me.

The man came around from the driver's seat, thinking I had more bags than the mere backpack I had on me. He towered over me, but appeared mild mannered. I nervously nodded a hello.

"How was the trip? You doing okay?" he asked in a strange tongue. When I didn't respond, he typed something in his phone, and showed it to me. နေကောင်းလား.

Oh. In school, we learned about other people in different countries, but I couldn't imagine how else anyone would communicate.

I nodded, though I seriously, seriously needed fresh air. The slow rumble of the train and all the people around me stifled my lungs. Instead of saying anything, I got in the car. The drive swirled 'round and 'round miles of mountainous terrain, fields of wheat, cities: small and large; I didn't know how I'd get home had I tried.

"If the men at the border ask you anything, just nod," the man spoke into his phone, which I guess repeated what he said in the language I understand. The men at the border wore a deep green uniform; they did not have guns on them, but they looked like they could easily kill me. The man driving me showed him important looking papers. One of the soldiers nodded, letting us through.

"Ruili," said the driver, pointing at the gateway we were passing through at the border.

Nearly sixteen hours later, when we got to our final destination, a woman greeted me. She must have had a thousand different colors on her, coruscating as she moved toward me. She smiled, giving me the same sense of comfort I felt when I was at that bookstore. Like I could breathe.

"Welcome," announced Mrs. Norzin, opening her arms wide.

I looked down at my feet.

The main building where the office and dining area were located was constructed more gallantly than anything I'd ever beheld. Long wooden tables, the height of my thigh, scattered the dining area. My eyes traveled an endless road as it looked from the tables with white flowers on the side (they would later be described to me as lotus), to the red walls decorated in five different exquisite patterns, up to the ceiling.

Mrs. Norzin showed me to my cabin—a room I shared with three others. As I walked to my bed, I noticed a woman staring at me. She said nothing, only stared. Did I do something wrong? I looked down at my feet again.

I soon fell asleep to the unfamiliar smell of a soup they make with noodles and vegetables. They later told me they called it *thenthuk*.

* * *

pg. 2: a new start

in this midst of all these noises
noises coming out of their mouths
it all seems a blur
a wild flux of sounds
a deranged flurry of tones
i know they're communicating
i know they know what's going on
i know they understand each other
au contraire to
me

in the midst of these new faces
foreign faces i am invisible to
it all seems obscure
out of focus
i don't know how to differentiate whether i'm
    the one without glasses
or they're moving by too fast
the only constant
has been Mrs. Norzin's bright smile
every time she sees me
she speaks slowly
not like i'm stupid
in a kind way
as if she could just as well be learning from me
she gestures widely
animating this strange environment for me to understand

i've almost started to believe:
believe life could get better
believe in the affliction of hope

in my past,
hope was not the thing with feathers, never
had it ever perched above me for a while
i would've stared up at it from the bottom of my well
an anomaly it would be
it would've laughed, ridiculing me for my nearsightedness:
"do you not see? what more this life could be?"
oh no, not me
and deadliest the Rattlesnake comes
and delighted it must be
that could engulf the little Frog

that could end its misery
I've heard it in the middle of the Amazon
and
really,
hope was the thing that stripped clean my gills
carved them right off of me
hope was the thing that sucked dry the moisture on my skin
oh no it didn't stop there
it cut all the way across my throat
i had three ways i could breathe
and it stripped them all from me

humanity

―

Bhinnêka tunggal ika tan hana dharma mangrwa
—CANTO 139, KAKAWIN SUTASOMA BY MPU TANTULAR

Idalia

I hate bulk. I hate having extra, just, *stuff*. After our round of visiting friends and relatives we hadn't seen in years, we cleared out a few suitcases of gifts and tossed the empty suitcases at my uncle and aunt's house. I felt lighter only carrying a capsule wardrobe of basics and my skincare products. Could've thrown it all out. But for my stupid vanity.

I was hit with fatigue when the plane landed in Guilin. Dismissing all the people selling souvenirs at the airport, I might not have had the best attitude saying no. Whether I should buy something I didn't need when one of the sellers looked like they needed money did cross my mind, but I hate carrying *stuff*.

My parents' money doesn't fall from trees, I justified after saying no thank you to an old grandma, hunched over with desperation.

Kindness is a habit, the angel on my shoulder argued, *practice it.*

What am I supposed to do with a crown of flowers that'll wilt in an hour?

Buy the lady a meal? angel suggested.

They're all asking, I can't afford to buy all of them a meal, I thought, glancing at the people coming up to us every few steps.

I've stopped saying I'm from America when they ask. I've read stories where ring leaders recruit the poor, the handicapped, and children to beg or ramp up sympathy for them, and at the end of the day they strip the desolate of their measly income from tourists. It's an industry: the target market is tourists; the marketing is how desperate the beggar looks.

In the face of reality, *is there still room for kindness?* Certainly there has to be because why else would the human race live on?

Guilin, breathtaking in beauty and named after the cassia tree, blossoms into gold when autumn comes. Known for the fusion of its mountain and river scenes, I cried watching a live amphitheater performance, "Impression: Third Sister Liu." Except it wasn't exactly an amphitheater; with mountains as its backdrop and a river as its stage, it was the first of its kind. Encapsulating a reminiscent local way of life, "Third Sister Liu" was directed by Zhang Yimou, legendary director of the 2008 Olympics. I was crying out of sheer awe of his talent. The timing. The music. The story performed using folk ballads. Broadway, take notes.

I was sitting in a bamboo raft flowing down Li River when I first noticed the shapes of the mountains. They quite literally resemble poop. Maybe we were better off admiring from afar.

"Hey guys, look: these mountains are shaped like piles of poop," I pointed out.

"She's not ... wrong ...," said my aunt, squinting.

"Will you shut up," my mom sighed. She had been lying supine on the raft, eyes closed in a faint smile, imagining what heaven is like.

"Will you shut up," my dad sighed. He was drafting a poem, wondering about the ethnic minorities that lived there (Zhuang and Yao people) before the Qin army invaded.

"I mean ... they do. Look at them," I continued.

"Seriously Idalia, shut up," said Legend. He was going through a breakup, and his ex would've come with us had he not broken up with her weeks ago.

No sooner had I ended my words did raindrops start drizzling: my eyelids, my cheeks, my neck, imprinting on my baby blue skirt until it grudgingly turned into splotches of cobalt. I smiled, petrichor filling my lungs. Soft and gentle raindrops fell, pitter-pattering their way onto the bamboo raft, drawing echoing circles all around me. As the mountains reflected a rich green onto the water the way it always has, as the reeds around us slightly bent under the pressure of the rain, Beethoven's "Moonlight Sonata" started playing in my mind.

I added my own lyrics.

And then I shut up.

After leaving Guilin, we flew back to Chengdu, where we originally stopped. From there, travel within Sichuan was by land. Sichuan felt like a home I never got to know; the cities never failed to amaze me with their fiery excitement; the people never failed to fascinate me with their straightforward fury, their open kindness. We drove until we didn't want to anymore, then from there we took a bus into the mountains. This bus swirled us around till I was knocked out dizzy, waking up as it aggressively turned onto an avenue, which led to a vast grass field jutting outside a large lake.

Not a trace of human civilization besides a wooden "welcome home" sign nailed to a tree greeted us at the entrance.

Underneath a deep blue sky were flocks of rainbow sheep. Their fur was painted shades of bright blue, green, red, orange—every color you could possibly see. Locals told me it's to differentiate which flock belongs to whom. As we headed closer, pleasant little cottages decorated by garlands of flowers sprung up from the earth as if rocks could grow; smoke twirled upwards from their metal chimneys, a hazy sky their backdrop as they danced around the mysterious myths they held. I thought I walked into a fairy-tale.

Grazing freely in the field were a herd of handsome horses, fifty shades of brown. Two white ones and a few black ones stood out boldly. I couldn't take my eyes off of them.

Farther along the field, three "cowboys" fled toward our direction in a hurricane. I couldn't believe they were real! As everyone around me bustled about, animatedly getting off the bus, all fatigue forgotten, I was afraid to move. I was afraid if I blinked everything would be gone. I was afraid if I moved tears would fall out.

Because the last time I arrived at somewhere like this was in my dreams.

I stepped out into a Tibetan homestay.

I'd always admired the redolent spirit of those stereotypical barbarous tribes who, historically, had grown up on horseback. Every time I think of the Mongolians or Tibetans, I think they are the epitome of free, bold, wild, zealous, and real. Unrestricted by the systems and institutions city folks suffer under. Some may declare that the minorities I'm thinking of are the ones deprived of a college education, dealing with poverty and social exclusion, economically marginalized, oppressed (the Chinese government was to Tibetans as the American government was to Native Americans. Was? Is?); they might declare that I'm clearly naïve and don't know anything about the world.

They might be right.

But I couldn't escape what I felt and can't un-see what I saw.

I might go back years later and think, *how stupid of me*. But right then, it was about the spirit that runs deep into their being.

It's who their ancestors are; it's who *they* are.

They keep their culture in their traditions; it has been ingrained in their language, and language inadvertently influences how we think. In their eyes, I saw this kind of contentment that marked a stark contrast to the wearied frenzy of people from the city. And people like me.

* * *

pg. 14

I'm stricken by the warmth I feel of people around here ...

In theory, there should be boundaries between my family and theirs, no? Culture, language, religion, way of life, way of thinking ... all these factors should've dumped a wall between us. We communicated in Chinese—they have an evident accent. They see us as whitewashed Christians; we don't understand Buddhism. Capitalistic America instilled in us a sense that life has to be go, go, go, climb higher, make more money, figure it out, be number one. It's a critical mindset to feed its citizens in order to sustain its market economy. With our standing in history, this mindset has proven useful, getting us to where we stand today. But to them, days stretch longer than twenty-four hours and there is time—time to dance and time to laugh, time to make bonfires and talk about the day. Time to milk the cows and water the garden. Time to enjoy. Time to stay simple.

yet as soon as we met, we were simply human together. nothing held us back from such deep and genuine connection. in those moments, our foremost identity was our humanity.

they laugh
boisterously
as if the earth had opened up and swallowed
their worries whole
they shout
loudly
as if it was their last day on earth and they were
heading into enlightenment
they sing
naturally
and all the birds would stop to listen

they dance
joyously
and all my soul could not fathom this could be a way of life
it is

I got in trouble when I was younger for running, jumping, climbing around in public and not being "civilized" or "respectful." If either of my parents told me more than three times to "get off of that" or "walk" or "smile" and I didn't do it, the consequences included kneeling on the ground for thirty minutes to an hour as punishment. Okay just kidding, I'm being dramatic. Ninety-nine percent of the time me getting in that much trouble was because I was arguing. One time it was two whole freakin' hours because I kept lying about bullying this little girl. I deserved it. No doubt it was for my own good, no doubt to instill respect in me. But there's a repercussion to everything.

As for mine? I hide behind the words respect, manners, refinement; I hide behind my perception of what others may judge me with— but how can they seem to be this free but still treat each person with respect and all the same? That's what I wanted to know. That's what I intend to find out.

* * *

With nothing else left to write, I looked up from my journal, hands smeared in black ink, smiling as Zion walked by our table with our uncle. My dad, working on a field report next to me, handed me his jacket. I didn't need to tell him I was cold and Mom was in the grass field miles away with Legend, our room key in her purse.

"What's up," nodded Zion.

"What'd y'all do?" I questioned.

"Swing."

"There's a huge swing over there—wanna come?" asked my uncle.

"Bet!" I shouted, completely unnecessarily, but enthusiasm boiled in my veins those days.

Lately, I'd been saying yes instead of no. I'd been ending my sentences on a higher note than they started with. I'd been delirious with joy. In the days ahead, I became so in-tune with myself, so encircled in by the mountains surrounding us, I had forgotten where we were. I had forgotten the time. I had forgotten who *I* was. And I was at peace.

I closed my eyes, taking a breath of this brisk forest air flourishing with life. Shh, listen closely. I heard the sound of animals I could not identify. Crickets, cicadas, did fireflies live there as well? I heard something between a hoot and a chirp.

Zebra? I've never in my life heard what a zebra sounds like. And if I do see them here, it'd also be around the time I see them fly.

Not only did lush forests paint the jagged mountains deep shades of green, nirvana enveloped them as well. The lake underneath, a product created by centuries upon centuries of erosion, veered off into a river that held strong and fast currents in the summer when snow melted most.

Jun, one of the hosts, warned us to "Be careful by the lake. A guy was seriously injured there recently."

"How so?" my mom asked.

"It's not the current that's the issue. He fell in and it took too long to get him back out. It's freezing in there. Water inside is melted snow from the mountaintops," Jun explained.

"How cold is it?" I was curious to test it myself.

"You wanna try?" Jun joked, raising his brows.

"I do."

"Okay, if you stick your feet in there for three minutes your entire family gets free housing. The entire time."

I jumped up, screaming, "I'll do it!"

"Idalia!" my mom, uncle, and grandma called at the same time.

"You'll thank me later!" I laughed, running to the lake.

They, in fact, did not thank me later. Not even a "nice try." Only three "I told you so" glares, mocking my freezing toes.

he got me

Arno

Flash forward: one year and 334 days later.

"Listen to me," I talked to Google as I stared into the officer's eyes. Trying my best to pierce through them. What is he thinking? Does he understand my urgency? Probably not because it made him nervous—his eyes started darting all over the room as if he were the one caught.

"Suppose you just *know* you had to help this girl out. Whatever the risk. There are certain things you don't have the words to explain. You *know*," I struggled to elucidate. The officer looked at me in confusion, like that was never a dilemma he'd had his entire life. *Ugh. What do I say? How can I describe it? Come on words, words, words.*

I slowed down, trying a more objective approach. Taking a sip of water, I tried to imagine how I'd be convinced if I was him. Okay, okay. Chief of police in a village no one really cared about; earned a dead salary that didn't pay much but had lots of say in local affairs; probably took bribes; this village was lucky to even have a police department here—most do not; singlehandedly responsible for five or so villages—technically overworked and underpaid if he did his job; mostly operated on a—"minimum effort, keep my job" type of way. How would I be convinced to help two troublemakers disrupting my flow?

"I'm from the States," I told him.

He sat up a fraction of a millimeter straighter, but he also rolled his eyes a fraction of a millimeter back. "An American. Overconfident, overweight, and over here. What are you doing here? Trying to save the world?"

He caught me off guard. Maybe that was a bad start. I meant to use my country to put some pressure on him. That was the class I should've been taking: negotiation, not whatever the heck I was doing. I scratched my head, trying to think.

"I was never trying to save the world—I'm here to learn from the world, sir," I clarified in a more humble tone.

I was trying to verbalize why I cared about Dolkar, but even I couldn't understand. Perhaps it wasn't even about her, perhaps it was about me. What was an argument he'd be persuaded by? An argument toward knowing you had to take action?

Spotting the jerseys he had hung up on a bookshelf behind him, I had an idea. After a few seconds of silence, I started again. "Okay, let me put it like this: think sports gambling. NBA, World Cup, NFL, whichever. You have magic. You're a wizard. You fight goblins in your free time or whatever. Point is, imagine you can predict the future. You *know*. So you happen to know which team is winning—are you gonna sit on your ass and lay eggs when you can predict the outcome? No. You find yourself a bookie and you put money where it makes returns. Right?"

He sighed, like that was the most ridiculous thing he heard all day. "You want me to pretend. *Imagine?*" he asked, rolling his eyes. I discreetly opened my hands up on the table—the slightest chance he might trust me a bit more. Doubtful though. I was in the middle of attacking someone ten minutes ago.

"Humor me," I said.

"What?" he asked. That probably didn't translate right. *Damn this language barrier.*

"This girl is being abused. Anyone with eyes and ears will tell you it's the truth."

"I know. We all know. It's not uncommon around here."

How could he be so nonchalant about it? That stopped my train of thought.

"Why didn't you do something about it?" I finally asked.

"There are five villages under our department. Six thousand people. Happens all the time. We don't wash our dirty linen in public," he stated indifferently. "Police don't intervene in family affairs. He's her legal spouse."

This information made my previously boiled blood, then having started to cool off, heat up again. I tried to tell myself that culture should be treated equally, I did. I tried. I repeated it to myself no less than a thousand times in the brief period I'd gotten to know Dolkar. I tried to tell myself that my own culture is deeply flawed, that not all domestic violence cases have good endings, that I'd directly witnessed our flaws in my own neighborhood numerous times. But I'd also grown to appreciate our mighty-powerful optimism. That optimism drove records: Wall Street rallies, NASA's milestones, a government for the people. I wouldn't be sitting there sticking my nose in Dolkar's business had I not stuck by my optimism.

"Then let me. Let her leave with me."

"You are not Superman, kid. Go home. Quit causing a nuisance. The only reason I'm not charging you with anything is because you have an American passport and the legal procedure to do anything to you is more tedious than necessary. Go home while I'm still in this mood."

"Officer, please. I'm begging you. She *has* to get out of there. Ask her. Don't you care what she has to say?"

"Frankly, I don't. Do you just *like* trouble?"

"It's your job!" I nearly shouted, slamming my fists on the table. Remembering the situation I was in though, I immediately held my hands up, palms facing him as an apology. I waited for him to nod before continuing, "If you won't do it, at least let me. I'll pay for everything. I'll get her somewhere safe—a nonprofit, a bigger city, anywhere but here."

"How do I know you're not a human trafficker?"

That stumped me. His point was not invalid: how could I prove I wasn't?

He let me leave, but warned me that if I tried anything under his watch, I'd be crying for my mom after he was through with me.

Before walking out of the station, everything clicked as I saw Dolkar's husband in a police uniform. Of course the police cruiser would have been waiting for us in perfect timing. Of course they wouldn't do anything about it; he was one of their own.

no sir we are not doing this

Idalia

Zion, Legend, and I were led to the stable by one of the cowboys. He introduced us to the first horse we saw as Snow White, who had this grace and symmetric perfection to her, like Grecian art, like Michelangelo's "David." Even her coat was glowing. I thought this made her too elegant for an unworthy rider, like me. The guy did not take no for an answer.

"She suits you," he said, matter-of-fact.

"If you insist," I supposed aloud, too eager to start running I couldn't bother to ask him to switch out Snow White. Then to Snow White I said, "Sorry, please humor me for a while."

After asking for her permission (I guessed her arched neck bending downwards meant it was fine), I hopped on. For once, I felt like a queen.

Both Legend and Zion were laughing at me.

"You two, race me!" I shouted from across the field, louder than I ever dared to speak.

"Learn how to walk before you fly!" my uncle hollered.

I laughed at everything all together and nothing at all. It was a place where it didn't matter if I was "too loud" or "too obnoxious"—it was quite simply an honest me surrounded by beautiful horses, open land, clear water, astounding mountains. I am nothing; I am everything. This was immaculate. My laughter was real: the loud, genuine type that comes from your soul.

For once, I felt free.

The guy who led Snow White moved with a quiet confidence, confidence that was encoded in his DNA and certainty that said he could move mountains had that been his choice of command. As if sensing my observation, he turned around, and with a curious glance he looked into my eyes.

It stopped my lungs in its tracks. He did not look away. All at once, it seemed important not to shrink at his presence. I lifted my chin high and eventually came up with, "I'm happy to be here; it's unlike anything I've ever known."

"Me too," he replied. His eyes—strikingly clear, cool, and intelligent—were eyes that could pierce through the façades of all of Wall Street combined.

All of a sudden, I was as naked as daylight and as open as a children's book.

"You what?" I asked innocently. *Doesn't he live here?*

He had the audacity to wink before turning away. I rolled my eyes. *No. We are not doing this. Not here.*

Would we be doing this elsewhere?

No! No puny little human emotions, end of discussion. Look, look at the earth and all its majesty: that's what you're here for.

You are human after all.

Which part of no do you not understand, Idalia? The—I'm leaving in three days—part, or the—he looks like someone who will break my heart—part.
You can't judge him like that.
I'm not judging him; I'm reading him. He's probably practiced reticence on dozens of women before you.
Read him better. He's bleeding passion. He's living the life you want to live.
Can you stop. Why am I like this? Wherever that reticence came from, it will not work on me.
His eyes, those eyes, did you see them? Intelligent and kind. Where have you seen that before? Oh, nowhere, that's where.
Shut it.
His smile. The way he chatted with your parents—charmed them off their feet. He was watching you the second you stepped off the bus.
I am charming. No need for him to think so; it is simply a fact. There are seven billion people in the world, half of them are men and he's not the only one charmed by me. Think about something else for goodness' sake.

So I thought about math. And I thought about wombats. And I thought about golf. And Tiger Woods and James Bond. And then I thought about my grandparents. And I thought about God. And contentment. *I think He meant for me to be content; I'm never content. I think He wants me to live simply; I'm a complicated mess.* Those people, those Tibetans living off the land and tourists, they didn't know the God I knew, but they lived in a way that reminded me of what heaven might be like; at least they seemed to be far closer to it than I was.

And then I thought about my best friend Ynez, how madly I admired her, how jealous I was of her, and if I really lived a simple, soft, content life, I'd never be like her.

Ynez happened to be the exact opposite of me: gorgeous to say the least, but also talented, eloquent, larger than life. She not only made the junior Olympics, but also owned an e-commerce business selling her own ceramics, loved physics and coding, and ran a popular fitness blog. If I absolutely had to point out a weakness, it'd be her insensitivity to the feelings of everyone around her. She was sharp in her speech. Sometimes, she talked, talked, talked, never stopping to observe how people were taking in what she was saying. That's most likely how we became best friends. She talked too much, and I listened so well.

The last time we talked, Ynez was doing research with a physics professor on astrophysics and cosmology, dark matter theory. As a freshman in college! Even though she took no part in the cosmological simulations, the fact that she was smart enough to be in the lab was already impressive. Standardized testing always came naturally to her; it never did for me. She said research was like having to find the questions that are to be tested for yourself, then testing them out not knowing if they were asking the right questions, and never arriving at the "right" answer. It all sounded like mush to me.

She confessed that she did feel like a machine sometimes, chugging along, never stopping for a break. But then again, she felt like she owed it to the Black hands that had bled through thorns in fields of cotton under the toxic Southern sunlight in the dead of summer, feet chained, voices forced shut, wars fought, the shoulders upon which she stood on, to blast down those walls of prejudice. She personally owed it to the generations before her. Only when she had a platform would she be able to make things happen. Only after she played their games would she be able to redefine the game with her rules.

I told her she was my parents' ideal child.

"Chinese food all day, bet!" she'd exclaim.

I told her all about the food here. I said it was like my mom's, but more flavor and more of it. Spicy was my mom's signature. Noodles were my dad's. We talked about the spicy hotpots that exploded in flavor around the dinner table, melting away all tension, the mundane-looking noodles saturated with garlic and oil and spices that make you faint, the steamed fish, steamed buns, and pork belly. The list goes on. Steamed noodles, fried bread sticks, dear god. My mom stuffed Ynez with so much food every time she came by, she could go on for three days without.

Ynez always ate everything on her plate. She'd politely express her thanks and talk to my dad about their scientific interests. After they'd had a long discussion about coding or Euler or the like, I would give her the "we done yet?" look, and she'd understand that I was about to get a lecture from my dad if she didn't end the conversation.

He always said the same thing: "Idalia, what did I tell you about studying math? It's the building block to a majority of useful careers out there."

I would sigh, "Dad, I get it."

He'd continue, "I told you and told you and forced you and you never listen. You only ever did the bare minimum in school. Look at Ynez."

"I'll be fine."

"*Fine*," he would humph, "your math skills aren't even up to an elementary level in China."

And on it goes ...

"I'm sorry I can never live up to your standards!"

"Darn right you never live up to expectations—you can't even meet my bare minimum."

I'd run outside, slamming the door on my way.

"Don't worry about it, this happens constantly," I'd tell Ynez once we were outside.

"Sorry, I probably caused that."

"No, no, it happens without you too," I'd assure her.

We'd sit in the back of my dad's blue pickup in silence, watching the moon gradually appear brighter, contemplating another life.

"I'm serious about moving to your house—your dad loves me," I once told her.

"And he hates the fact that the last time I read a book for myself was in third grade quiet time," Ynez chattered offhandedly, swirling around a leaf in her hands.

We laughed together. Irony, irony, wherefore art thou irony?

Now, I didn't want to think about anything anymore. Instead, I took the reins from the cowboy, turned Snow White around, and took off. Or Snow White took off, at my command. Every time I squeezed my thighs, she went faster.

"Go, Snow White, faster, love, go faster!"

That she did. Never have I ever flown that fast on a horse, not even in Texas. There, with Zephyrus echoing in my ear, Boreas storming up my hair, views caressing my sight, I was gone with the wind. My whole body bounced up and down, following Snow White's rhythm.

"Faster!" I screamed. I lost sight of the views; they all became a blur.

Snow White started taking matters into her own hands—or hoofs; in other words, I lost control.

"Whoa, stop," I tried, again and again. She either couldn't hear with that much wind or she didn't care to listen. I was holding on for dear life, waiting for her to tire herself out.

Please, please, please, please, please, make her stop, Lord I will die.

Snow White continued. I held on tighter.

Omigod, omigod, omigod, maybe if I say it thirty more times, she'll get the hint.

I shut my eyes tight. *She can't go on forever can she?* It took every muscle in my arms to hold on. I felt my grip slipping. It only felt like she was going faster. My hands were slick with sweat. My fingers were sliding from the reins.

Just when I thought my life was over, I felt Snow White jolt. Opening my eyes, I saw a lasso around her neck; she was still struggling to break free. Next to me was a man on a horse. Unfortunately, it was also the very man I did not want to see.

"Thank you," I managed to squeak, a little shaken.

Amusement was written all over his face. He said nothing.

"I'm okay," I volunteered.

"I know. Snow White wouldn't do anything insane unless you tell her to."

So it's my fault your horse went out of control. Granted, I started it. So maybe I deserved it, but that didn't stop me from getting annoyed. There, I let my emotions run as wild as my heart. Anywhere else, I would've acted nonchalant, I would've acted like I didn't have time to let my annoyance trouble other people. There, I forgot how to hide the emotions written on my face.

He suddenly let go of the lasso, and Snow White didn't wait for him to say go before she leapt into action, gaining back speed as swiftly as a Bugatti.

"You son of a ..." I started, unable to finish.

I waited, struggling to hold on but knowing that this time there was a solution.

The second time he lassoed Snow White in, I jumped off her once she slowed to a walk.

"Hey," he called after me, "I'm sorry."

I wanted to slap him. "I don't know how to ride. You're insane."

"I really thought you did; you were running so fast."

"Your *horse* was running so fast. Don't follow me," I demanded, walking faster, exasperation in my voice.

"Really, I'm sorry."

I continued walking. *The faster I get away from this piece of insanity the better off I'll be.*

He stopped his horse in front of me, holding out a hand. "It's too far to walk."

I ignored him, but he was right. I called my aunt, who had arrived at the resort later than us in her own car, to pick me up.

"Didn't you leave on a horse?"

"It went crazy. I don't want to ride her back."

I needed a drink.

* * *

Tibetans are big on hospitality, but it was astonishing to see how far their hospitality goes. It digs into their former nomadic lifestyle: since it was difficult to be traveling so far all the time, visitors were highly treasured. Back then, they lived in *drokpa*, black tents made from yak hair.

At dinner, cowboys came in to perform. The "ticket" to perform, they said, was for a volunteer to drink three shots with them.

"Me!" I shot up; heaven knew I needed this drink.

My eyes grew wide when they brought out the drinks. These were not shot glasses; they were more like mugs. Too late to sit back down.

I drank the way they did: bold and unrestrained, chugging it all the way without stopping for a breath.

Jun looked at me in approval, "好酒量" (nice tolerance level).

Of course, it was nothing in comparison to them; in reality, my tolerance was nonexistent. I was already tipsy; every woman has an inner actress. They later told me that the alcohol they served would traditionally (and even nowadays) be used for women to recover after childbirth, so the ABV was very low, and it had health benefits.

The boldness in their culture was reflected in the details of how they were raised. Jun casually put in that he started drinking (with permission) at three. Drinking: not to taste, but drinking as a drink.

During the tour Jun gave us, he introduced his lifestyle to us. During the seasons with the most visitors, they stayed at their homestay to work. During off-season, they traveled, mostly throughout Asia to make it in time for work.

"I'm so jealous," I expressed in awe.

"Would you trade lives?" he asked me.

"Depends on if I can bring my family. If everyone around me stays the same, but we get to live your lifestyle, I'd do it."

"I'd do it too. With your life."

Shocking. I didn't ask any other questions.

There were some stinging nettles growing on the side of the narrow path. Stinging nettles are miraculous plants—on contact, they cause an itchy/stinging/painful rash, but the plant can also be used as medicine.

"Man, my parents used to spank me with these plants if I was being bad—to be spanked by one of these, heck yeah you'll learn your lesson. For life."

I sure hoped my parents didn't hear that. Zion would be cursing this man in his sleep.

Later that evening, the resort had scheduled the event we'd been anticipating all week long: a traditional Tibetan bonfire. When dusk hit, everyone who worked there was bustling about, busier than bees, running back and forth in preparation. Plate after plate of traditional Tibetan food was laid out: yak meat, butter tea, momo (made of wheat flour, this dish resembles dumplings in filling, but is always accompanied by a special hot sauce made from tomatoes, chilies, and garlic), and of course *chhaang* (a popular alcoholic drink across Nepal and Tibet—tastes slightly sweet and fizzy and comes with texture from the remnants of rice or grain) were the only four basics I could identify. At last, they set up the two fires: one for roasting a whole lamb and another for the bonfire. Blazing wildly underneath a blanket of stars in their enigmatic winking, the bonfire represented the hope of all things lost: the idea that, sometime long ago there existed a camaraderie amongst humans who could not communicate with each other.

They even went so far as to lay out costumes for us to change into: beautiful and exquisite, the vibrant colors screamed to bring out the dauntless in me. I listened; in that space where no one really knows who I was, how hard could it be to redefine myself? That day, I was Dauntless herself. Well, almost. Every time I looked up across the fire, *that* guy had his eyes on me; I didn't even want to know his name—I didn't care to know. When our eyes met for the third time, and he still had the nerve to hold my gaze, I thought, *alright two can play*, and never looked down. I was dauntless, remember? Five seconds later, he raised his glass to a toast and poured the rest of the chhaang down his throat. I copied. With my water.

And then, without any sort of warning, he screamed out from across the fire, "You're ridiculously pretty!" People looked up from their conversations, looking around to wonder what was going on.

I did not copy that.

He was ridiculous. Better that he stop at ridiculous than say his whole sentence. I wanted to scream at him to *shut his fat mouth up*. My dad! Was right there! My mom! Was right there! My grandma, uncle, aunt, brothers! Were right there!

I ignored him, turning away.

"Is he talking to you?" Legend teased, loud enough for the world to hear.

"*You?*" Zion cried, like it was an absolute novelty his sister could be pretty to anyone.

"Y'all crushed pieces of cabbages. Shut up."

* * *

pg. 15

*I Am
content and
I need to
figure out how*

*why is it that
happiness is
harder than sadness*

and

contentment harder than loneliness

and

and

and

the desire to please everyone else stronger than the desire to please yourself

why?

* * *

The *how* consisted of staying there for a few more days to figure it out. When I tried explaining to my mom, she gave me the "mom look," arms akimbo.

"Mom, just tell me no if you don't want me to; I can't stand that look," I said.

She continued staring me down, like she knew something I didn't.

"Mom."

"Be safe," she said lightly, warning in her tone. I don't understand how she does it. I felt eight again.

"Okay, I love you."

I stayed because I needed to find the answer to my question: how?

How can these people be that reckless and free-spirited but also make everyone around them feel this respected? How come *their* recklessness doesn't contradict with respect and self-control? It did in my world. Or even still, how did they cultivate their happiness? I'd been taught my whole life that *I can't have both*—I either restrain myself and adapt to the desires of other people, or I do what I want and disrespect everyone else. I either practice self-control and accomplish much but reel in my feelings, or I let myself go and let myself feel, but accomplish nothing.

There *is* no win-win.

Is there?

the woman who would not stop staring

"*Aquilo que se faz por amor está sempre além do bem e do mal.*"

—FRIEDRICH NIETZSCHE

Dolkar

For a second, I woke up, unable to comprehend where I was. It was still dark outside. I rubbed my eyes, waiting for the familiar gnaw in my stomach. Weird—it never came.

If ever needed, I could show you a million ways to trick yourself into believing your belly was full when you're staring up at the hole in the ceiling in the middle of the night with your stomach growling during winter.

Lie upside down, head on the floor, legs on the bed. That way, you make yourself dizzy. Your stomach is propped directly on the edge of the bed. The pressure on it makes you forget about the hunger.

Boil roots and weeds to eat. Roots of any plant, roots of grass, trunks of smaller trees. Take some salt from the nearby sea. Season it. Realize it takes too much energy to walk miles to draw water when the pipes start to freeze. Stop seasoning things so you don't get thirsty as fast.

Eat the dead fish that have washed ashore.

This time, my stomach was full, even in the middle of the night.

I yawned, careful not to shuffle the plastic cover underneath me. I turned onto my side; the plastic did not make noise. I turned to my other side; the plastic did not make noise. Odd. I discovered what was underneath me was not a sheet of plastic but soft, real bed sheets! I could not believe my eyes or ears.

I sat up, waiting for the stench of the animals out back I'd been accustomed to. No such stench arrived. It smelled like nothing I'd ever smelled before. Lavender was the name of the air freshener they used; I was later told.

I drifted back to sleep, dreaming of blue skies and ruby cardinals.

I woke up again when the three other women got up. One was pretty, with a long black braid and strong, structured features. One was chubby, with rolls of fat like stacks of naan. One had cheeks the color of tomatoes. This time it was light, and I understood I was here to work for the Norzin family.

The woman who was staring at me the first day I arrived continued her staring. I did not know why. I did not know what to make of it. She was the pretty one.

Eventually, I found a routine. I did what I was told. While language was my biggest issue, life became quieter when I didn't understand anything. Moved slower. I was always in my thoughts, alone. Sometimes I didn't think. There is nothing left to think about when you've been in your own thoughts for hours. I liked the quiet. For the first time in my life, no one bothered me. No one knew my father. No one knew my mother left. I was just the new maid. I even went to bed with a full belly! Perhaps this was happiness.

I had spare money for the first time in my life. It always used to slip me by, never belonging to me.

The work was nothing more than what I was used to.

The pretty woman was the quietest of them all; I'd never heard her talk except to say "yes" very softly and ever so gently. One night, I was walking in from prepping the kitchen for the next morning when I heard her soft incantation of *parittas* in my language.

I laid down and waited till she was finished. "You speak Burmese?"

"Yes," she answered. "I'm Eindra."

I could barely hear her.

"How is your dad?" Eindra asked. She was brushing out her dark, luscious hair.

"He's good," I replied.

Is he?

"He still gambles?" she pressed further.

I was sleepy before, but I could no longer pretend I wasn't curious about her. I sat straight up. "You knew him?"

"Yes, I... I used to," Eindra suddenly seemed to regret starting the conversation.

"How did you get here?" I pressed on.

"A man named Mr. Han introduced me to Mr. Norzin and Mr. Ma."

I could barely recall, but it sounded like the same man father had talked about. It didn't take a genius to put two and two together: she lived in our village at one point in her life.

"Sleep now," she muttered softly, turning off the lights. Her parittas sounded like lullabies to me.

on authenticity

Idalia

I will always remember Hai-er, the woman who advised me to follow my heart, but I will also be cursing my heart for disagreeing with me. And then I will curse myself for not listening to my heart. And then someday I will die without seeing for myself what it was I wanted.

I called out in a singsong tone to Hai-er as she stood hanging white bed sheets out in the sun to dry. The sheets swayed softly with the wind, smelling like fresh grass with a dose of warm sunlight.

Hai-er, one of the owners of that resort, smiled abundantly, stopping what she was doing to wipe her hands on her apron. Her cheeks, the color of flamingos, naturally turned pink from years braving the mountain winds. Her luscious braids swept down to her butt. Adorned by a headdress ornamented in turquoise, yellow, and orange beads, she had maybe eighteen different colors on her all at once; I was wearing black, the same exact color I wore every day.

Beyond the pleasantries and telling me that she was born in Tibet and moved out at age nineteen, she was hesitant to talk about herself. I would've considered my attempt at conversing with Hai-er a complete train wreck had she not delved deeper when I asked her about her regrets.

"My grandparents passed away back home, and I didn't get to see either of them before they passed."

I didn't know where to go after the silence. I wanted to express my condolences, but since it's not common to convey this with "I'm sorry" in Chinese, I didn't know how to say the phrase in my own language. She broke the silence by asking me about my stay again; and in return, I asked her about this homestay idea.

"We try to keep everything as simple and traditional, as primitive, even, as possible. We produce raw honey, and we grow a vegetable garden out back. Our guests come from all over the world. Instead of buying a service, they're buying insight into our lives."

"I'm in love with this idea. The busyness of the city makes people want time to find themselves, time for a slower lifestyle, time to step back into the past. Your business precisely fits this desire," I complimented.

We talked about our families, food, and the small town.

Eventually, Hai-er sensed there was more to my seeking her out, so she gently stated, rather than asked, "Idalia, you're not here for small talk."

I gave it a few seconds before I figured out how to start the topic. Before I asked her about her lifestyle, though, I was curious about the Tibetan Sovereignty debate.

"Let's hear what it is," Hai-er prodded, nonchalant.

"The Tibetan Sovereignty Debate …" Though I was a minority at home in America, I was not a minority in the country of my birthright. My bloodline is of the Han Chinese. For Tibetans—and similarly with other autonomous regions with different people groups—even living in their own country had them answering to Beijing.

Hai-er explained thoughtfully. "I think we've relied on China for so long, it'd be onerous to be independent. With little to no status on the world stage, it's outrageous to try declaring it. At the same time, we don't have the same opportunities to assimilate as much as the CCP want us to, and they've gone back on their promises of autonomy numerous times. Some of the policies have seriously hurt our roots." She bent down to begin hanging her laundry again. I didn't want to take too much of her time, so I stepped forward to help, but she waved me off with a kind smile.

"How so?" I inquired instead.

"Well, language. Language is the soul of a culture," Hai-er started without thinking.

I nodded enthusiastically. It is truly powerful; I will never stop believing it has potential to make or break nations, empires, entire worlds. It's the one key I felt that colored the invisible hand—which, I think, at least for America, has been white.

"The implementation of Mandarin in schools, per se, is quite useful. It gives our children a way out if they wanted to start a career elsewhere. But what strips away our identity is *forbidding* the use of Tibetan altogether in elementary schools. They've enforced policies that stripped our teachers their jobs, implementing Chinese teachers in our local schools so there's no way Tibetan could be spoken unless parents teach it themselves. It disconnects children from their parents, and forces children to haggle over their identity."

"Was that what went on in your family?"

"Jun got to travel back to Tibet with us multiple times when my parents were alive and running this land. When my father passed away, we never had the time to teach Shang proper Tibetan or take him back. That foundational problem built up a wall between us; hurt and misunderstanding were the outcome."

Language was an added nuance to minority struggles in China that wasn't blaring America in the face—there were so many there that having one standard made sense.

I honed in on the answer I wanted from her all along. "The way I was raised, I feel like I have to live out everyone else's desires before my own. My parents are *good* at sticking to what's needed to survive, so anything radical I do would be disrespectful, even if they don't define it as such. If I were to follow my heart, if I were to let my heart decide, I'd be bordering selfish. But *you*—you're different in a way that I envy. Despite your widespread struggles with being a minority, your minds and lifestyles seem *free*, yet it feels conventional; it feels right. Tell me how you do it."

"I think," she looked me straight in the eye, "you already know the answer."

"What? But I don't ..." I grappled with myself.

"Idalia, find out for yourself. Follow your heart," Hai-er advised, leaving me hanging.

Follow my heart? *My* heart? *This* heart? It was too wild for my limited work ethic to back up. I'd stopped trusting it to make decisions for me a long time ago.

I was never good at standardized testing, but I'd like to think of myself slightly better at the test of life. *What if the blaring simplicity is the obvious answer?*

Back at square one, I walked along a path till I spotted a short wall separating the large green field from the cottages;

sitting down with my feet dangling, I started to think. Eventually one thought led to the next and looped me back to where I started. I came to the conclusion, for the time being, that authenticity takes conscious effort; it's a way of living, it's a lifestyle. Because living authentically requires you to, first and foremost, possess authenticity first. What does that mean?

You should know yourself; you should be clear on who you are, who you want to become, how you are to get there. At the same time, you should work on acquiring magnetic characteristics, the fundamental attributes that make people want to be around you. You can't simply walk around under the façade of being authentic if your pursuit is harmful.

The few things I got straight:

1. There's definitely a balance. The line you can't cross is having your authenticity hurt or undermine other people.
2. Authenticity requires conscious effort. It takes more effort than simply succumbing to "society."
3. If it's really what you aim to pursue, then your authenticity should be more valuable than what society deems as valuable. If you're going to walk around like a bully insulting everyone in your way, or lie around like a bum doing nothing all day, you might as well ditch your effort to go and seek what society deems as worthy: success, money, a perfect-seeming family, flawless-looking relationships, a house, a car, materialism, stability, etc. If it's more valuable than that, seek that authenticity. But what is value and how is that determined? (Maybe I didn't have this point cleared out yet.)

As my thoughts ran through an unending labyrinth, I noticed someone coming. *Him.* Go figure. He quietly sat down next to me. *Uninvited.*

"What's on your mind?" Lighting a cigarette, his sotto voce remark shrunk my thoughts to nothing.

Still gazing toward the pasture, I wrinkled my nose and brows. I hated the smell. I hated not being able to figure out life. I hated what he was doing to me. I made every last effort to make that conversation as dead as it could possibly be without being overtly rude about it.

"Nothing."

"Didn't seem like nothing to me."

"You interrupted."

"Sorry," he simply said as he gently put out the cigarette, "answer my question?"

"No," I said, monotone, though I liked how he noticed my discomfort with the cigarette. I hadn't mentioned it.

"My loss."

"Will you please leave me alone?"

"No."

I sighed.

He continued indifferently, "Try streamlining your thoughts out loud."

"Why?"

"Just curious," he shrugged.

"Reason's not good enough."

"Maybe I can help," he suggested.

"Not good enough," I echoed.

"Thinking out loud helps you navigate your thoughts."

"I don't need to navigate my thoughts." *It's not like it's a problem or dilemma; I've lived with it for as long as I can remember. It's not a big deal.*

It was actually the biggest deal of my life.
"Come on," he urged endearingly.
I don't remember the last time I made *go away* more obvious.
"Idalia," he said, a little impatient when I gave him no response.
"What?" I was still trying to act nonchalant, but I was astonished at how American his pronunciation of my name sounded. He never spoke of knowing any English.
"Why are you doing this to me?"
"What am I doing?"
"Look at me."
I turned around and glared at him.
"Give me a break. You are lovely to everyone here; the second I'm near, you turn cold. You radiate warmth and liveliness everywhere else; the second I show up, you shut off. Why?"
"No reason." What was I supposed to say? *I resent your type?*
"I don't think so," he shook his head. "I think you're intentionally making it so *damn* hard for me to flirt with you."
Took you three days to figure that out? Go work for Sherlock.

déjà vu

Arno

Flash forward: one year and 326 days later.

"Go back to your *respective* homes," the chief had emphasized, looking straight at me. I went back to the room I shared with Carlisle by mid-afternoon, completely dejected. All the energy knocked out of me. Carlisle, who came to this village to volunteer with me, kept asking what happened, how our master plan got hijacked, but I didn't feel like explaining. I needed to think. I plopped down on our bunk, feeling useless as two shits.

How am I not a human trafficker? How am I not a human trafficker? How am I not a human trafficker?

"Hey, how am I not a human trafficker?"

"What?" he was stunned.

"The officer. He asked me how he would know I'm not about to turn around and sell Dolkar," I answered.

"Psh … as if he cares," Carlisle shook his head.

"You're on point. He doesn't like trouble. In other words, he deadass lives for the paycheck. And us stirring a commotion in this village puts him on the map in front of his superiors."

We were stumped into silence. This whole thing was pointless. Who did I think I was? Spiderman? I would just swoop down and carry Dolkar away like that? From her legal *husband*? Who also happened to be one of them?

Screw this whole thing. *I hate how useless I am. I hate these people. The entire village doesn't give a crap, why should I care?* I was also hungry, so I got up to boil some water for ramen.

I thought back to the moments before we had packed our bags for this trip, while we were still on campus. And it made me think, *what in the actual hell. I really did not come here for this sentimental stuff. I came here for a summer because Carlisle dragged me all the way out here to volunteer, to teach English.*

The minute I stepped into the train station in China, I almost turned right back around to the States. The heat, the smells, everything was saying: get out of here, run as fast as you can. Sprint. You will be altogether miserable. And then there were the looks people gave me once we got to the village, a mix of awe and curiosity. It was like they'd never seen a foreigner before, and even more insane? A *Black* foreigner, *wow*. Most people looked away when they noticed me staring back. This one old lady literally stood there with her mouth open, gaping, as if she just witnessed Moses part the Red Sea. I stared back; she didn't look away. I smiled awkwardly; she kept her mouth open. I walked out of her way; she dropped her dead chicken.

Luckily for us, we had translators. Didn't know how else we could teach these kids; it'd be charades every day.

Otherwise, tell me, how do you mime out verbs? How 'bout you try first?

The first few days were rough, not gonna lie. Diarrhea almost killed me. Everything I ate immediately either came up or went down liquid form, and nothing digested right. Why was I here? Kids are weird. Like little creatures from outer space.

When the program directors arranged for us to head to the local market, to "seep into local culture," I jumped at the chance to stay back and take a nap.

"Yo, come on dude, you've been sleeping ten hours a day," Carlisle noted.

"So?" I answered, plopping down on my bed in our shared room.

"So, we should make the most of our month here."

"This place will be the death of me," I complained.

"You'll be fine once you get up. We could get you coffee, or aspirin." He didn't let me off very easily.

Carlisle couldn't take the hint: wicked smart, outrageously ambitious, great guy, but lacked social intuition. He eventually convinced me to go, don't ask how.

I slugged my way to the market, hating life, hating everything; who decided this was a good idea again? The market was the worst. The noises hurt my head, as if I weren't already tortured enough.

We bought cantaloupe. The program director had told us to bargain, explaining that that was what everyone did around there, but all I could say was *xie-xie* (thank you). The woman selling the cantaloupe held up two fingers, then rounded her other hand into a zero. Twenty. I held up a one and a five. She shook her head, and I gave her my money. That was about the extent of my "bargaining" skills.

We saw "fresh" fish. Straight from the sea. Or the lake. Or whatever that huge body of water was. I didn't care. It was supposedly a "seep into local culture" experience. All I could experience was my splitting headache. I felt like I'd been slugging around behind them for eternities. I was about to head back to our room myself and ditch them all.

> *But then I saw her.*
> *We locked eyes.*
> *And I couldn't look away.*

I only later learned her name: Dolkar. It was like déjà vu confronted me from my walking dead state. I stood there for a solid five minutes before Carlisle shouted from across the market that we were leaving.

I was reminded of my own past when I saw her, the skinny, battered, tattered girl walking slowly behind the fat woman who turned around every minute to check on her. A ghost of a figure, she walked around like life was sucked out of her. It probably was: how and by whom, I wondered till the darkness of dawn.

If it wasn't for my world history teacher, I would've been stuck in a similar situation. I didn't know what kind of similar situation. I just knew it was hopeless. I just knew she had no way out.

I *knew* because I'd *been*.

* * *

pg. 1

Hell,
I cannot get the eyes of the girl at the marketplace out of my mind!
I cannot describe the depth of what those eyes told in unspoken words.
All I can say is—they mirrored what used to look like mine.
I imagine only someone who possessed what those eyes told could truly see what lies in them there's this empty hopelessness in them I can't describe
beyond a—why is this happening to me?
it ventured toward a—I deserve this, I accept this—territory
I will not get out of here until I find out what's going on because
if not me, who?
if not now, when?

how many more

Idalia

Instead of replying, I got up to leave. This was pointless, actually. Some things are better kept unsaid. *Does he ever think beyond the moment? What are our chances of forever? Less than one percent?*
I'd been conditioned, ossified to protect my heart fiercely. *Did you not see the way he looks at you? One kiss wouldn't have killed you.*
Shut up, me.
I know, I know he never meant any more than exactly what he said. He purely stated whatever the truth that was currently on his mind was. *His* truth. I knew Tibetan culture raised kids to be outright and speak their mind. I was raised to be reserved, observe what's going on, and determine my actions and words based on the dynamic and what's at stake. I was raised to assess the situation; he was raised to say it as it is.
Live a little.

I pondered for a moment, wondering whether letting him break my heart would be worth the fun. Wasn't Voltaire the one who said illusion is the first of all pleasures?

So illude love, and then leave with nothing but a gentle flick of your sleeves.

Illusion or not, no means no. I'm leaving tomorrow.

Why are you so uptight? Are you aspiring to be a nun? No one's asking you to be a saint.

You really think I have the tenacity to be careless? Who do you think you are? I know myself—I wear my heart on my sleeves. That whole "leaving with nothing but a gentle flick of your sleeves"? It would fling my heart out there to die. I know that starting anything would give him the leverage to break my heart. I have to protect myself.

You would not mind getting your heart broken if he were the one breaking it.

I hate you.

Later that night, once in bed, I tossed and turned for hours, my thoughts altogether strangling and suffocating the sleep in me.

The more irritated I became the stuffier the room felt—I couldn't take it anymore. I stomped outside, strolling along the mud path I was on earlier. I sat down somewhere random and, using the moonlight, I sketched out horses. It started to rain. I sat still, drinking it in. It cleared out my thoughts, and I was a free woman again. The rain sprinkled my page with its random splotches that bled out the ink, giving my ugly sketch watercolor-like qualities, marking its territory on my page. The rain advised me to "Stop trying. Let me take over. When you let the universe into your art and it becomes more than yourself, then no matter how it turns out, it's alive."

Stop trying. Stop trying to be someone you're not. Stop trying. Stop trying to fit into a mold not designated for you. Stop, just stop …

* * *

pg. 16

how many times does my heart have to fall from my throat to my stomach, back up and down again
how many times do I have to listen to 《三十岁的女人》, 《一个人的北京》, and 《座位》
how many times do I have to write and rewrite, edit and reedit my career plan
how many times do I have to buy my own flowers

> *watch the moon and drink alone*
> *wait for the sunrise and dance*
> *on my own*

how many more trips do I need to go on alone

> *enjoying every second but afraid of*
> *dark lonely nights*

how many more amusement park rides do I need to sit by a stranger on

> *obsessed with exhilaration but wishing*
> *someone could share my excitement*

how many more prayers do I need to pray

    stories of "it didn't work out" do I
        need to tell

how many more times do I need to write "true love awaits" on my wrist as a reminder of how strongly I will resist their versions of love

    as a reminder that maybe, somewhere,
        my version of love exists

how many more wrinkles or scars do I need to get
how many more problems do I need to solve myself

        before
        you,
      love of my life,
      come into my life

how many more times can I believe in love at first sight?
or rather, that love can be pinpointed down from just a few interactions

    before I give up on my whole philosophy
        altogether
        and die
      having never loved
      or been loved
    the way I want to love
      and be loved?

explosion of stars

Dolkar

With summer afloat, sweetness gyrated in the air, diffusing a thick foam of humidity that hung in our lungs. We invited anyone who could breathe to our first festival celebrating the heaviest travel season. All day long, we were running in and out of the kitchen like ants before a harsh winter. We brought out plates and plates of beef, lamb, fish, and chicken prepared in every way possible: steamed, fried, sautéed, roasted, broiled, stir-fried. I couldn't get enough of the smell of fresh herbs. Vegetables, picked fresh from the garden, were drizzled in all kinds of sauces: oyster, light soy, dark soy, mushroom soy, tamari, chili oil, sesame oil, gochujang. Sweets and delicacies I imagined sit at the table of England's queen decorated the table in notes of pastel. Star of the night? A whole lamb. Rubbed in chili and salt, it roasted slowly above an open flame. Mrs. Norzin's son flipped the lamb around the skewer every few minutes. I looked down at the dish I was carrying, burning red, as soon as he looked up.

Guests were especially interesting because they all spoke incongruously. To me, it sounded like a cacophony of tones and noises, but to them, it *meant* something. The variety! Absurdity! Vespertine hour arose; when we got off for the night, all the maids went back to their cabins. I lingered, wanting to listen to them a while longer.

"Dolkar, come join us," called Mrs. Norzin, pulling out the chair next to her.

I pointed at myself—*me?* No, no. I looked at Mr. Norzin, and he nodded with enthusiasm. Hesitating, I still felt like I shouldn't be sitting with them.

She gestured for me to come as she leaned over her husband to grab a clean plate. My steps dawdled back and forth until she got up, walked to me, gently took my hand, and didn't look satisfied till I sat down and started eating.

Carefully tasting a drink that exploded like little stars in my mouth each time I took a sip, I sat back to enjoy, noticing all my nerves disappearing. Colored in a soft pink I thought would be alluringly sweet, I was surprised to discover the strength of its explosion. Perfection. This was the best meal I'd had my entire life. If only my dad could see me now; if only my mom could. Maybe if she knew this was where I would be, she wouldn't have left. Then again, if she knew why I was there in the first place, maybe she'd have left sooner.

That night, I couldn't've been more satisfied. Fascinated, I rested my chin on my hands, listening. Harmony was most definitely not the goal; I smiled, hearing people sing at the top of their lungs around the fire. The mellifluous sounds would escalate into my dreams that night, and I'd start to think:

All along, this is where I belonged?

Zeus please, just go

Idalia

A bath. That's what I needed. I needed the steam to get rid of my thoughts. Focusing as much as I could on the hot, rose-scented water, it was not lost on me that the steam was not enough to stop my wandering mind.

If I don't leave, this place will surely be the death of me. I should've gone with my family. My mom was right, like always. I'm trying not to think about him, but it's just so hard. He's been on my mind nonstop—from the first wink, to the lasso situation, to that genuine laugh, to the way he interacted with my family, to his confidence that never *ever* approached cocky, to his simple, straightforward approach to life, to …

Idalia, you are one hell of a woman. You're amazing. You're kind. You're courageous. You … I tried convincing myself.

To his washboard abs … the whole package is hot as hell. The way his mesmerizing eyes dance when he laughs. And that night he got mad at me, the way he locked his jaw. God. I would've kissed him right then and there had my name not been Idalia. How he towers over me, how he seems to notice my every move, always believing there are volumes of stories to me I have yet to tell him, believing in my extraordinary-ness when *I* don't even believe it, seeing me more clearly than I see myself.

Shut up.

Two knocks at the door interrupted my thoughts. I peered through the curtain at the window, straight into his eyes.

Mother of God. Speak of the devil, there he manifests himself. Why was he here in the middle of the night? I turned and began walking away, letting the curtain drop.

"I need five minutes," he called as I crawled back into bed.

I laid there and ignored him for five minutes. All he did was stand there quietly. If it hadn't been for his shadow through the curtain, I would have thought he went away.

Since he didn't say anything more, I should have just left it at that. Let him think I fell asleep. Except that I didn't.

I'm insane, I thought, as I padded back across the floor, opening the door drowsily. *I have officially lost all reason.*

"Hey, you're leaving tomorrow?" he asked simply.

"How'd you know?"

"I check the finances."

Oh. I had totaled up my bill with Jun's father, Mr. Ma, earlier. I just stood there and stared at him.

"I'm Tashi."

"Nice to meet you."

"I came to say goodbye."

"Bye," I said, closing the door.

A hand stopped it, and along with that came a comment that sounded like, "You play a risky game."

I rolled my eyes and crossed my arms.

He sighed. "Maybe I saw wrong. Maybe the fervor was another façade of yours. Maybe you *are* cold-hearted."

My eyes flickered in anger; perhaps it was unwarranted, maybe it was the alcohol, regardless of what it was, he had no right. Game! What game! I'd never in my life participated in modern dating! I was acting cold for the sake of both of us, did he not understand? He should've taken the hint! How dare he label me as cold-hearted. Cold-hearted would kiss him and leave him out to dry; cold-hearted would not restrain herself the way I had done. I hated his stupid label on me. Labels meant constraints—the antonym of everything I sought after. It was too late to act like I didn't care; he already saw the heat in my eyes.

He got the reaction he wanted from me.

I lost my composure. "What do you want then? What. Do. You. Want? For me to flirt back, for us to hook up?" I gestured in exasperation. "We don't belong in the same world. Get out of my sight. I mean look at us: we can't even have a decent conversation witho—"

He didn't let me finish; his lips were on my open mouth, fire and ice. His insistent mouth sought my trembling lips as I fought myself hard. He ran his hands down my jawline, to my throat, finally resting on my waist as I registered what was happening. I forgot that I was supposed to be fighting myself because that's how good he was. I tasted like ice, and he smelled like sin.

He stopped, bracing a forearm against the wall above my head. "Couldn't let you go without doing the only thing I've thought about since the first time I heard you laugh," he whispered under his breath.

"I knew it," I smiled tensely.

"Let *go* of your self-possessed dignity, how wrong would it be to let yourself feel for once?" he mumbled in my ear.

I looked up at him nervously, shaking a little bit. Inhaling, I continued. "I don't ... I ... I mean I've never ..." I struggled, gesturing to him, then to me.

He humored me, surprise and amusement enveloping his eyes as he smiled, realizing what I meant. He shook his head in disbelief. "A woman this enchanting has never ..." he paused, laughing. "Okay, follow—I mean copy—me."

I turned into liquid gold. Follow him? Where? *You have only to say my name, and I'll follow you to the ends of the earth.*

Slowly, gradually, I knew I was doing more than just *not kissing him back*; I lost to myself: before what was happening synced with my brain, I was kissing him back with a destructive force I couldn't comprehend. The tension was so thick and electricity so fierce we felt the world fade away as the sky split open—Zeus himself must've come down to see this, curious as to why there was a greater force, there of all places. I grabbed Tashi harder, closer to me, legs wrapping around his waist.

He groaned, low in his throat as he shut the door behind him. He held me tight as we gave in to our passion. Zeus realized it was only a kiss, and left as he saw Tashi become more and more gentle. He started tasting: tasting the faint magnolia that was my scent and the bit of Hana Lychee Sake on my breath.

"Someone's been naughty," he whispered hoarsely.

I laughed. "It's sake, do you want some?"

"I had some."

My blush was all the response he needed as he kissed me lightly on the forehead, lingering, as if saying *I promise I care. I know you feel like you fall for the wrong guys, but for you, never. I'll fall in love with you, only you, and I will be both your comfort place and your craziest adventure, mark my words.*

* * *

Tashi led me outside, sitting down on the couch next to my room.

"It's cold, can we go inside?" I complained.

"No."

"Why?"

"Because there is a bed inside. Let's not tempt ourselves, please."

I laughed; he liked it. A lot.

"Pretty sure it's just you. *I* can control myself," I noted.

"Aw, man. Thought we were getting somewhere," he chuckled before turning serious. "Can we talk?"

"Okay." I nervously sucked in a breath as I waited for him to start.

Tashi took a while to gather his thoughts before continuing. "Let me tell you what I'm thinking: I won't ever force you or, or persuade you to do anything more, but I couldn't let you go without laying things out in the open. I know you don't think it's possible for us to be together ... I see our differences as well as anyone—but I want to try. I can't promise you anything ... but I'm willing to try long distance with you. The choice is yours."

I hesitated, knowing even if we tried, things would end badly. I watched my parents struggle with faith; I couldn't repeat their mistake. They were crazy about each other; they made it through all these years, but their fundamental difference was still their faith.

All the jokes gone wrong, all the insensitivity, the fights, I didn't believe they'd ever work. I didn't say anything for a long, long time. We sat still for a long, long time. I was shivering, less from the cold than from what I was about to say. He put his arms around me; I slowly shook them off and pushed him away—*I can't be attached*, I thought, as I realized what I had just done with him. Good luck forgetting *that* one.

"Tell me. I'm ready for it," he finally said, quietly under his breath.

"I …" I choked, trying to look up.

He gently wiped my tears away. "It's okay, I understand."

But more tears came. He waited.

As we sat under the blanket of stars, I started telling him my parents' story. And for the first time ever, I met someone who was a better listener than me, someone who asked the right questions, who was curious without going overboard. I told of how in love they were, how they built a world together, how compatible their personalities were—my mom was fire, my dad was ice; she brought out the best in him, he grounded her.

"She's passionate about life. She brings life with her wherever she goes. He's passive, intelligent, philosophical sometimes," I explained, looking away from Tashi's gaze as I tucked a stray hair behind my ear.

How my mom became captivated by Christianity, how my dad was quick to believe but also quick to leave our faith, how many fights that very foundational problem provoked, how every fight they'd ever had stemmed from that problem.

It always started small: after my mom donated more money than she usually did to church and said she needed to donate that amount because she felt the urge from God, an insensitive joke from my dad along the lines of "Huh, God's using some darn modern marketing" could spur fights that lasted days. My dad keeping me at home to study Chinese when I should've been at church could make my mom become so belligerent she'd start chucking things at him. Heavy things.

Another time, I stole a piece of candy from one of those dispensers you're supposed to weigh and pay at the checkout when I was maybe five or six; I genuinely thought they were for customers to take because don't restaurants give customers candy to take home at the end of your meal? An H-E-B employee saw me and scolded me for stealing. My parents ended up in a Cold War for weeks, blaming each other for not bringing up their child right, my mom saying it was because my dad didn't teach from the Bible, my dad saying what's the point of God if you bring up such a child?

I never stole again.

Eventually, I ran out of things to say; Tashi ran out of arguments to make; we were about to part ways when he came up with one more way to keep me.

"Happy families are all alike; but each unhappy family is unhappy in its own way," he quoted.

"Implication?" I asked.

He explained, "We all want to be both happy and unique. If we were to all be happy, we'd all be alike. To want to be unique is to accept unhappiness—in ourselves and our families."

"Tashi, I don't need philosophy from Tolstoy right now."

"What I'm trying to say is, we could be struggling with something else if this wasn't our struggle. Everyone is risking *something* ... but only with great risk comes great reward. Since we'll always be struggling with something, why not go for it regardless?"

I admit—that was a heck of a good argument. It took me quite a while, more than a while, to come up with a rebuttal.

"Because we *know* what the great hamartia is in all men," I paused, "and women. We think that as long as we achieve our greatest wish, we'll be happy. Not ... to be presumptuous, but for conversation's sake, let's say yours is me. You get me. For a year, I am everything you've ever dreamed of. I am exciting. Then, you start to realize how, let's say, vain I can be. Or how selfish. Or how I never discuss my decisions with you. Or whatever it is. And you might fire back at me with something like—I thought you were Christian. I thought you were supposed to be obedient. But I'm human—I'll always be struggling between self and ideal."

I paused for a second, thinking I didn't know how to round this back to the point.

I continued, "And because we already know what it is we'll be struggling with, that doesn't eliminate all the other struggles we don't know. All we're doing is optimizing the risk with no chance of a greater reward."

"You're *everything* I've ever dreamed of huh?" he said, sounding serious. What a tease.

I rolled my eyes.

"If I were to use an example, I'd use a realistic one," Tashi continued.

I didn't know how to win that one. "You are *really* not helping your case, man. You are *really* acting like someone who will never, *ever* have a chance of kissing me again."

Holy, why did I say that?

"Did I have a chance before I said that?"

"No."

"See?"

"Back to my point: I'm not what you want," I asserted.

"Yes, you are. I think I've seen enough of people to say that I know what I want."

"You're not what *I* want."

I had flipped things around to where he couldn't say anything to that one, so he continued with Tolstoy, "That's why he also said 'if you look for perfection you'll never be content.' Never would I ever *expect* perfection."

"I thought you said you'd respect my decision. Let's not end this with ..." I paused, trying to come up with a way to word my thoughts. "With you 'looking at me like a man looks at a faded flower he has plucked, in which he can barely recognize the beauty that had made him pluck and destroy it,'" I finally quoted.

After a long time, he said "You're right, I'm sorry."

We sat in more silence before he started again. "Since this was our 'make it or break it,' will you tell me about your God?"

"Yeah. Hmm ... where should I start?"

"Maybe start with love. I know Christians emphasize love."

I glimpsed at him inquisitively. He explained how, in 2008, back when there were all these violent uprisings in Tibet against the CCP, his parents sent him to a private Christian academy in New York for several years to keep him safe if anything ever got out of control. At the time, protesters chose 2008 as the moment to protest Chinese hegemony because the Olympics would shift international attention over to Beijing; so as to not have the CCP downplay what was going on, violence erupted in Lhasa, the capital of Tibet. Buddhist *monks* were setting fire to Han Chinese-owned businesses. The outrage must have been way beyond breaking point for protests to be organized by monks.

They heard gunshots from their homes—for China, for Tibet, gunfire was *rare*. To say it was bad would be a ludicrous understatement.

Tashi ended his explanation, "Go on with your Christianity."

"Where do I start? A lot of atheists know way more about the concepts than I do."

ZEUS PLEASE, JUST GO · 155

"Well, I was on my phone every time they brought this up, never paid attention. I also couldn't understand anything in the very beginning."

I laughed, of course he hadn't paid attention. "Love. My relationship with Jesus starts with love."

"Jesus?"

"So you *really* didn't pay attention. We believe our God is one God with three forms: the Father, the Son, and the Holy Spirit. Jesus is the name of the Son—He's the one that walked on this earth."

"Oh, that's simple, I remember that."

"So ... God created man in His own image for companionship. When man sinned, he could no longer walk with God because God is holy—He can't condone sin. Because God loves man, He decided He wasn't going to destroy everything and start over. He sent His Son Jesus to die on the cross to atone for man's sin. Because of His death and resurrection, we are able to enjoy God's presence again," I elucidated.

"Resurrection?"

"Jesus died on the cross, and then He came back to life after three days. He experienced all the joy and pain, temptations and emotions, of being human. He then rose up into heaven to be with the Father again. And so, for me, He's like a friend most of the time. It's a working relationship. He's always faithful, I'm always not. But I always know of His forgiveness, and I always try to do better because I love Him too, just not nearly enough."

"How do you know this is real? How do you know you have it right?" Tashi asked thoughtfully.

"I don't. At least not for the human race. I just know it's right ... for me. It's real ... for me. And the only reason I want to share it is not because I think I have it more right than anyone else—it's because it's the most precious gift I could ever give anyone. And it's free."

"That's what faith is right? You know for yourself this is the Truth, but you can't prove it to anyone else," I summarized.

"Ah."

"Yeah ... anyways, I wish you nothing but the best."

"You too, love." Tashi winked.

"You are *not* allowed to call me that!" I exclaimed.

He just laughed. "Goodnight."

I went inside, turned off the lights, and tried to go to bed. It wasn't till five or six that I finally dozed off, plagued with that familiar dream. In my dream, there was a plum blossom. One single plum blossom. Me. There was also a precipice, with a man standing on it. Below it, desperation everywhere. It seemed like a drought had taken over the land. People were starving, kids were dying, it was another year with no harvest. Wind blew, knocking off the plum blossom to its death. I was roaring at the man to do something about the children before I fell to my death, *I* wanted to do something, but no one heard me; I was a puny plum blossom. I always woke up sweating, screaming for someone to free me so I could pick up the wailing child crying right before my eyes.

I woke up at 8:05 a.m., dead tired. The bus would leave at 8:15 a.m. I couldn't wait for the water to get hot before stepping in the shower, throwing on some gray Drew sweats—the only sweats I owned—leaving my hair wet, and sprinting out the door. I caught the bus just in time. Good thing I didn't have time to be nostalgic.

I picked a spot in the back and sat down, ready for a new adventure. Xi'an? A city chosen by the founders of thirteen dynasties, was it shining just for me? Inner Mongolia, wait for me. Hangzhou? Yunnan? Jiangnan? A city that attracted the souls of artists and poets alike, was it calling my name (Jiangnan doesn't actually exist as a city nowadays, but it was the name they used in ancient literature).

That's when I spotted him, Ray Bans propped on his nose, white t-shirt, leaning by a fence, watching the bus drive off. My heart was dancing.

"Stop!" I heard someone blurt out to the bus-driver.

et tu Brute

Arno

Flash back: three years ago.

I really thought my only escape route at the time was death. Out of all of the numerous choices I had (namely, two), death would've been the optimal one.

    I lived near Seven Mile Road in Detroit, Michigan. Long ago, it was described as a place that powered the engine of the American dream, but nowadays, it was a place foul with decay. Even police dared not tread at night. There, violent crime was five times higher than the rest of the country.

    "Hey, you mind if I borrow that?" I asked the redhead next to me in world history, pointing to her spare pencil. This was the one class I actually wanted to pay attention in.

    "Yo, why you keep sounding white like that?" the person in front of me turned around to ask.

    I didn't know how to answer. Frankly, I'd never thought about it. Sound white how? I grew up in the suburbs, and when my mom left my dad for "something more," Dad and I moved downtown.

"Et tu, Brute" I remember screaming at my mom the last time I talked to her. She kept sending us money, but even that was not enough to cover the bills. I never took another call from her.

All the damn medical bills, man. We had to give up our house in the suburbs and move into one my grandparents left for my dad. The zoning explained the schools. Overworked, burnt out teachers. Dirty supplies. The like. There was a $200 million deficit in the school system at the time, I was later told, if that puts things in perspective.

Our bills kept adding up, so I got a job at this place called A-town Burgers. The restaurant was massive, built to resemble the seventies: checkered floors, red tables, greasy everything. After hours of monotonous flipping, hours of mindless frying, I was ready to scream. But still, I would walk the twenty minutes home from my late 10 p.m. shift Tuesdays and Thursdays every week. If I had done that for the rest of my life, I think I would quite literally be brain dead. I wasn't using my brain enough. Or at all.

That Tuesday night, we racked things up, wiped down everything, and got ready to go. I stood outside for a few minutes, breathing in the fresh air. I didn't want to see another burger my entire life.

"You need a ride?" a man I had never seen called out from his bright green Mustang, turning the music down. The type of music that makes you churn. Heavy metal. After my double shifts, it was the kind of music that made me want to throw up. Maybe throwing up would wash away the repulsive smell of the fast food I'd been smelling for the past eight hours.

"I'm good, thank you," I called back, walking faster.

"As you wish," he said indifferently.

On Wednesday, he was there again, smoking outside. My shift ended earlier, at seven, so I got to see him clearly. Saggy pants, tight white shirt. Tough, bulky build, massive biceps, highlighted by his sleeve. Minimalist characters dotted his forearm and what looked like birds and frogs around his shoulders. Seemed nice enough.

He nodded at me; I nodded back. I continued walking.

For a few months, life became a blur. I accepted that first cigarette from the dude in the green Mustang. Called himself Heist. Creative, though couldn't imagine parents naming their child *Heist*. He definitely made that one up. And why not take his offer? It was just a cigarette. After six hours of flipping burgers, I needed a kick. Of something, anything.

Then I tried something stronger. Showed up to work high. No one could tell, it was fine. It got me through my day.

I started riding with Heist when he'd stop around the corner for gas. Dude's chill. Quiet, but chill. I thought we were friends.

"You wanna get outta that life?" he asked one day when we were out back smoking.

"What life?"

"School, work, your purposeless, robotic, repetitive life."

And yours is purposeful? I immediately thought. Glancing at his arms, I figured it would not bode well for me to say something like that out loud. I paused, unable to answer. In reality, I didn't have time to think much about it. Things were getting worse at home. Dad—his hands were starting to shake, and we had no one to take care of him. I had bills to pay.

"I'm okay—I need the money," I answered.

"How much?"

"What?" I asked, surprised by this follow up.
"How much money do you need?"
"Why?" I repeated myself.
"Do you need the money or not goddammit?" he said, his voice rising, all signs of patience gone.
"No," I replied, heading back to work.
I didn't see him for another month.

idiocy

"A ship in harbor is safe, but that is not what ships are built for."

—JOHN A. SHEDD

Idalia

"Please stop!" the obnoxious person screamed, running to the front. "Sorry!"

The bus driver grunted, opening up the doors for this idiot. Who was she?

Hold on. That was *my* voice? What was *that*? What had I done? I didn't recognize my own voice. But I had to have been the one who stopped the bus driver, for I was the only one who got off, sprinting toward Tashi's open arms.

"Welcome back," Tashi commented, ever so leisurely.

I didn't know what I was doing; I mean, I could barely register who this mad woman directing my action was. I stepped away to call Legend. His calm was always infectious for me. It worked magic: every time I panicked over something I knew was trivial in the long run, he was always able to calm me down. I wish Legend were right next to me. Then I could deal with anything.

"What's up?" Legend answered.

I stuttered. "I ... uh, I ..."

"You kissed that Tashi guy?"

Of course my brother would know. Nothing he said was helpful, only his voice. I needed that; he doesn't know. I left him on a *what-the-heck-did-she-call-me-for* note as I turned back to Tashi.

"Listen," Tashi started, turning serious. "Listen to me." He stopped, lifting up my chin to make sure I held his gaze. "Promise me you'll let yourself love. That phrase sounds absolutely *ridiculous*, but I mean it."

In response, I blushed crimson at his touch.

lullaby-like parittas

Dolkar

Contract and pencils. I saw a long contract and four pencils lying on a desk. An army official stood over my dad as I stood on his other side; I straightened the four pencils into one line, handing my dad the sharpest one.

"Pen only," the army official ordered. "Blue or black ink."

We didn't own pens. I looked around frantically. The official took one out of his shirt pocket, handing it to my dad. It was clad in something shiny, embossed with a metal cap and, as my dad signed his name, I watched in envy as I saw how smoothly the ink came out: liquid silk.

I glanced at the content of the contract a minute too late. I saw the status of the army official, knowing he was above the police. I was prevented from calling the police for help. *Why would I need to call for help?* I wondered as I skipped a few lines down and caught words like *brain, operation, revenue*.

Each voluntary operation would be compensated in the amount of ... I didn't see the number before the official snatched the contract away.

Next, I was taken to a hospital, bigger and cleaner and fancier than anything I'd seen my entire life. They strapped me down as doctors began shaving my hair.

"No!" I raged, squirming to get out of the table they strapped me in. "No!"

Wordlessly, more doctors came in to hold me down. When I felt like I couldn't fight them any longer, a woman burst into the operation room, screaming at them to let me go.

"Don't touch her!" the woman exploded, a mop in her hands, threatening to hit anyone who didn't get off of me.

Eindra? Why would she be here?

My dad came in, stone-faced and silent. He grasped Eindra tightly, telling her to calm down. "It's just a quick operation; she'll be fine."

Eindra's words turned into venom, a stark contrast from her usually gentle demeanor. "A coward. I married nothing but a coward. They are experimenting with my daughter's brain and you have the *audacity* to tell me she'll be *fine?*"

I jolted up from my dream, screaming for my mom.

Eindra, sitting up from the bed next to mine, frowned slightly. "How did you know?"

you can't have me

Tashi and Idalia

The week flew by faster than any week had ever flown. They never had a routine. As promised, Idalia let herself fall in love: in the way Tashi's voice sounded in the morning, beneath the fuchsia aurora as Snow White galloped and they bounced. In the down-to-earth way he was friends with everyone, between times he set for work and for her. In the way he believed in her, more than she had ever believed in herself. He could now pinpoint why she made him want to try anything, to *be* anything for her: she made his world more hopeful with her sincere eudaemonia. She argued that he was just calling her naïve, but she was wrong. Her sincerity was one backed up by her values. She had this innate ability to ... he couldn't form it into words in either Tibetan, English, or Chinese. *Je ne sais quoi.*

What Idalia had was uniquely hers. It wasn't a marketable skill—it was a vibe, a scent, a personal perfume, a gift she carried with her from heaven. Whatever it was, it was electrifying, a flavor of brandy just for him. Whatever they talked about, he admired how she formed her ideas into words, how she looked when she was deep in her thoughts, appreciated her curiosity. He loved how easily she took his jokes, never taking herself too seriously. He respected the way she treated people. *People*, all people.

Wednesday, she came down to lunch in a white silk slip, an aesthete stepping right out of Vogue, rosy, excited, and glowing.

Holy Buddha.

That day happened to be one where an entire tour bus came to the dining area at once; it was packed with suitcases, servers running around, people everywhere. Tashi got up to straighten out an issue they had at the office, something about a cash flow problem due to a recent payroll payout. As he was walking back to the dining area, he saw Dolkar, a new employee, running over with a pot of tea to refill a customer's teacup at the table next to theirs. She turned around to leave, tripped over a pair of white Converse as she left the table, and spilled the rest of the tea directly on Idalia. The other customer shot up and had already stormed directly to the office, tired and cranky from his trip, and angry that there were this many people in a homestay advertised as a relaxing, calming experience. By the time Tashi ran over, the situation was already chaotic.

Dolkar was tear-stained, as this was the first time she'd been less than the most hardworking employee here, and she had already been yelled at plenty of times by this impatient customer.

"Sorry, I'm so sorry," Dolkar kept repeating.

Idalia was shocked at first. Then she calmly smiled, put on Tashi's jacket, and got up.

"How memorable," she laughed, soaking wet.

She proceeded to calm Dolkar, looked around for a tissue, couldn't find one, and handed her a napkin. When she didn't take it, Idalia wiped Dolkar's tears away herself.

"It's okay. You're doing well. Maybe you could go wash your face in the bathroom and take a few minutes. Then breathe, it's going to be a great day. I'll deal with this," Idalia comforted.

Idalia was wiping down the table as Tashi came back with ice and towels.

"Let me do it," he said, handing her the ice. Glancing at her arm, his brows furrowed, his eyes full of concern. They kept black tea at eighty-five degrees Celsius; he prayed this one had been a neglected pot.

Idalia had class. Real class. Not feigned class that usually comes with a finicky attitude he saw in customers all the time. They came in flashy clothes, asked loudly for the most expensive things on the menu, told their friends the meal was on them, and the whole homestay held an unspoken consensus, wishing for their disappearance. Not her. She was the quintessence of class.

* * *

Idalia consistently insisted she was fine, and that ice was enough. Tashi said nothing, dragged her into his Jeep, put on her seat belt (with her blabbering the entire time), closed the passenger door, and went to the driver's seat to take her to the pharmacy.

"Which part of I'm fine can you not comprehend," Idalia grumbled.

"You *are* fine," Tashi emphasized.

"I am," she echoed, detached. It took a few seconds to register. Quite a few more seconds. "Oh. Ha, ha."

"Are you sure your college accepted you? What if they made a mistake? Check with them again."

"You know what, I just might. And while I'm at it, I'll see if there's a class called 'Lame Jokes 101'."

"What are you studying there?" Tashi questioned.

A flash of emotion darkened her features, there and gone in a split second. "Eyes on the road," she warned without taking her own eyes off the road.

He thought that was a perfectly reasonable question. "What do you *want* to be studying?" he rephrased.

Her face lit up, and it was even harder to look away from her. It did not go unnoticed that it was too late to stop his mind from wandering down the many unacademic paths ...

"Spanish. French. German. And Greek! Hebrew. Korean. Japanese. Every language in the world. Even more Chinese. Dude! Did you know that in Indonesian 'thank you' translated directly means 'receive love'? Isn't that fascinating? Oh, and the classics! I've never read *The Odyssey* in its entirety, and I've heard people tell me Odysseus and I have the same fatal flaw." Her voice rose octaves higher, her face was aglow with suppressed passion, and he knew he'd hit the right subject.

"Stubbornness?" Tashi joked.

She laughed; she laughed so often these days.

"What would you do with all those languages?"

"Oh, I would travel! I'd look for ways to integrate into local culture, and I'd open tea shops and start orphanages where I felt the need. I could do so much!"

He didn't doubt that she would. "Where would you go first?"

"Nepal. Or Croatia. Japan or Argentina! Wherever the wind takes me."

"Why?" he wondered.

"I read this book, *Little Princes* by Conor Grennan, and it hit me in all the right places; it was set in Nepal, and I wanted to go help out badly. Croatia because legend says Aphrodite, goddess of love and beauty, was born at Petra tou Romiou in Paphos. And definitely the Sahara Desert."

"Sahara Desert?"

"My favorite author lived there! I'd love to do what she did, but I'm also afraid of everything she encountered there. It's one of the only places I wouldn't go alone."

"Do you want to go now? I'll come with," Tashi suggested casually.

Idalia actually considered it for a split second. Tashi didn't have the heart to point out to her that maybe she needed to either have a trust fund or at least an income before she tried any of that. Her hands gesturing wildly, he imagined a thunderstorm billowing from within her.

He liked her, simple as that.

He liked them, simple as that.

* * *

Tashi had to go to the office to balance out the accounts before the season ended. As they sat there with his ledgers spread around the table and Idalia's *Wuthering Heights* in her hands, he didn't dare think about when she would have to leave at the end of the two weeks. Their time together had been so seamless, so easy, so fitting to imagine it had always been and would always be like this.

Idalia asked what Tashi was doing, so he tried explaining it to her. It made perfect sense to him, and he liked doing it, but she furrowed her brows in confusion when he pointed out the accounts on the ledger. The simplest way he could explain it was with a balance sheet.

"Look. There's assets, debt, and equity. If you subtract what you have, assets, with what you owe other people, debt, you're left with your net worth, or equity." He drew it out into a t-chart, assets on the left, debt and equity on the right. "Everything, cash flow, risk, all originate from the asset side," he pointed out. "Then finance comes in and messes with the debt and equity."

"Simple enough. Why does it look so complicated when you're doing it?"

So he tried to go into taxes, depreciation, paying his employees as well as their investment in a new facility in Vietnam. Their income came from multiple sources: the obvious, but also their raw honey, organic vegetables, their rental land, and investments. He had to budget out the marketing for the new facility.

He lost her at his description of all the different types of depreciation, she thought, picking up her copy of *Wuthering Heights* again. Cathy had just passed away in her book when she drifted off to sleep on the beige couch in the small office with warm lighting, Yiruma's gentle piano melody, and the smell of black coffee. She woke with the familiar screaming, the same old dream plaguing her, except this time she rolled off the couch and fell in Tashi's arms, with him tenderly murmuring her name.

"Idalia."

"What just ... oh, I'm sorry."

"Don't be, what is it?" he asked.

"Nothing." She liked how he sensed that she didn't want to continue. She was slightly embarrassed—it wouldn't even count as a nightmare. "What time is it?" she asked groggily.

"Almost three. Let's go back to your room, you'll catch a cold here."

* * *

Lightly kissing her goodnight, Tashi lingered till Idalia not only smelled his faint cologne, but could list out all the top, heart, and base notes of it. She was still shivering.

"Let me stay a little longer," he whispered into her mouth, caressing her through her clothes in a way she thought was more scandalous than if he just took it all off.

"Why me?" she asked.

"What?" He knew exactly what she meant.

"You're clearly experienced, more than I could ever be."

"I ... will use my whole life to show you why it has to be you," he said seriously, his eyes piercing right into her soul.

"Just kiss me," she moaned in a low tone, eternal flames leaping in her eyes.

He spared no time as he took her body in his arms, turning her up on his. Had he done anything but, he would've been in pain. *She's beautiful*, he thought, *she's perfect*, as fascinating as a hurricane, like the turmoil surrounding Helen of Troy wrecking through his logic; her flawless skin exactly the way he imagined it'd feel, their bodies intertwined like they were made for each other.

Her last scintilla of reserve vanished this time as she lost herself in the kiss, boldly kissing him back with everything she had. When Yale rejected her, she thought she had lost all recklessness. But as she knotted his hair in her hands, moving her body with his, running her hands down his abs, the recklessness came back as if it had never left. The feel of his controlled strength sent chills up her spine. He turned her on her back, hands slowly searching up and between her thighs.

It took every last bit of discipline to tear herself away from him.

No. "Please," he leaned in again. He tried fastening his mouth to hers, but she turned her head slightly, and his kiss landed on her neck.

"Idalia."

"Stop," she panted.

He cocked his head in confusion. "Did I do something wrong?"

"No, no you didn't. That's my limit."

"Your dress is still on, everything is still on," he pointed out, still confused, as if this were a foreign concept.

"It should be." She blushed, sitting up. She tucked her hair behind her ear and shyly lowered her gaze, not knowing it drove him crazy whenever she did that.

They sat in silence for a while before he finally asked, "So no sex at all?"

"No, not never. Just not before marriage."

"What?" he exclaimed, as if that were the most exotic idea he'd ever heard.

"Does that make you want me less?"

"Absolutely not."

"Then why are you so shocked?"

"Because ..." he hesitated.

"Because you've already done it before," she finished for him, her gut instinct telling her the answer way before she asked.

"Twice," he clarified.

"Oh," was all she could say. She always thought her boyfriend should've saved himself for her just like she was doing for her husband. She thought that was only fair. She thought her first serious boyfriend would *be* her husband.

"Does that bother you?"

"Yes," she said softly, sadly, honestly.

"Hey, oh my God don't, love," he rambled, thinking words would make the awkward silence less awkward. "Don't let it bother you, okay? It's been four or five years, no exaggeration. I was eighteen and nineteen."

"I'm *fine*, just naïve," she snapped through gritted teeth.

"Idalia, you're mad. Don't be," he pleaded.

"I am. I won't hide it. And I *know* I'm being unreasonable, but I can't stop myself from thinking about you with someone else. Whoever she is. And you can't stop me from being mad when … when *I* can't even stop myself," she argued, throwing her hands up in exasperation.

She paused, calmer now, continuing with, "And I *want* to, believe me, I *want* to be careless and act like it doesn't bother me and throw away my virginity like it's an act of liberation … it does make a statement if you're empowered by it. But I can't. I'm conditioned. I'm mad. Please leave so I don't say something I can't take back."

"I don't even *remember* them. A weekend in downtown Manhattan after getting drunk with some friends. The other one's a shadow in my thoughts, my girlfriend from high school—we were stupid and drunk that night too. I would understand if you're mad because I'm forcing you to do something you don't want to, but I'm not. I'd never. I just can't understand you holding my past against me." Tashi gestured, still patiently explaining though in a progressively less even tone.

"I can't reason out why I'm mad. There's no logic to it. And you still remember the sex though; you can't forget that."

He sighed. "Fuck the sex, it's you I want!"

"Yeah, well, I can't give *me* to you. You can't have me, any part of me," Idalia remarked with cool resolve.

"I'm not *asking* for your virginity! I'm asking you to be reasonable," he pleaded.

"Can't, sorry. *Go*," she insisted, starting to push him out.

"Goodnight," he finally said, bending down to kiss her on the forehead as she dodged it, mildly slamming the door in his face.

Idalia knew she was acting immature; she knew she was being petty and unreasonable; she couldn't let go of the picture in her mind, and how *drastic* a contrast it stood against her idea of what her first relationship would look like. She was annoyed—annoyed he'd started it, annoyed at herself, annoyed at the world. She hated that she was right at first, and then he came and casually tore down her walls. Red flags shot up everywhere she looked. In fact, they weren't flags: they were glaring lights.

Tashi stood outside her door, dejected, all the energy suddenly knocked out of him. He knew she was too good, too pure, far too innocent for him. She still wore rose-tinted glasses, while his had long turned clear, perhaps even a little darker than clear—he hadn't seen the color rose in so long he forgot what it looked like, forgot he still had the capacity to see joy the way she did.

Joy: she was full of it. He shouldn't have let her fall for him. She was probably right in acting so heartless when they first met. When they first met. She'd had her eyes on the horizon, so focused and so lofty. He wanted to strip down her pride. Because it seemed like passion was screaming to breathe from within her, and she wouldn't let it. She kept herself self-possessed. She kept her cool, but inside she was crumbling. She only let her heart sing for a second, that second he winked at her; her mask fell, and so did he.

He knew damn well he should let the flower keep its radiance for itself.

When another man came along, someone who saved himself just for her, their union would be glorious, heavenly. Angels singing. Trumpets galore. What was *he* doing? Why the actual *hell* was he intervening? The right thing to do would be to call it off altogether; it hadn't even been a week, neither of them had sunk in very deeply. Right now was the perfect time to say, hey it was fun, but we're not right for each other. She knew that, she knew that way before he realized it; she'd *thank* him if he were to end it.

Now, the truth of it is glaring him in the face: they weren't right for each other. *She's too good. Pure.* Not in a way that was derogatory toward him, rather in a way that was as true as it gets. He used to hate being around those "good girls," heads tilted high, thinking they were better than everyone else just because of their upbringing. She was ... wild. *She doesn't fit in anywhere—she is her own self.*

And yet, *yet*, at the bottom of his soul resided a selfish creature who tore through all the goodness he could muster. The creature ate away at his logic, enveloping his thoughts in *the* most primitive way: he *wanted* her for himself. Not just the sex—though he wanted that especially—but her body, mind, soul. The creature couldn't think beyond the present moment; it reasoned that his enchantment toward her warranted such a price. Bloody Naraka. Why was she saving herself for "the one," for her husband? That was almost a blatant statement that it wouldn't be him. Why not? Why couldn't it? He'd drown her in his genuine love; sex would be a natural outpouring of her passionate love in return. *What's so wrong about that?*

*Yeah, well, I can't give **me** to you. You can't have me, any part of me.*

Why not?

welcome

Arno

Flash back: three years, two weeks, and six days ago.

I couldn't tell you what was going on had I tried. Next thing I knew, I was throwing up in a dark alleyway full of colorful graffiti. Dozens of motorcycle headlights punctured the dark. A punch in the stomach sent my insides churning. I took off sprinting faster than I ever had my entire life. Faster than you have your entire life. Faster than you ever will; faster than your mom, your dog, or your great grandmother's ghost. Usain Bolt might have had trouble keeping up. Not that it mattered, because once I reached the end of the alley, I realized I was cornered by a group of people all wearing balaclavas and chains. I backed up slowly into the corner, panting, eyeing the guy stepping forward.

"What do you want?" I tried to keep my voice steady and calm despite the obvious fear rising in my chest. My heart was racing. Nothing in my life ever prepared me for a situation like this. I would rather face a wild animal. Grizzly bear or two; that way, I at least knew why they were attacking me. Might be protecting its young, might think I'm a threat, very rarely would it attack to eat me.

This attack had no reason.

"Too good for money?" someone asked.

What was he *talking* about? I looked around, quickly attempting to scurry up the chained gate. My last chance. Too slow. That guy tugged me down.

"Not so fast," he taunted, throwing several punches into my ribs. That did it. The fried chicken I ate thirty minutes ago came up, spraying all over his face. I took the chance to run the other way, crumbling right into the arms of another guy in a mask. This one had a baseball bat he refrained from using.

Instead, they all crowded closer. Multiple baseball bats. We must've been behind some bar because crates and crates of glass beer bottles were stacked up by the side of the wall.

"Give it to him," voices echoed, cheering.

I was a game. One of the guys would throw a bottle up, another would bat it toward my direction. Was anyone keeping score?

Them: 8. Me: 0. I thought as another piece hit my thigh.

I quit trying to run away; I covered my face, sheltering my head, but that didn't stop bits and pieces of glass from hitting everywhere else. Sharp shards of it dotted my back; I could feel the warm blood dripping through my shirt and onto the concrete. I didn't know what I'd done to be in this situation.

I laid there on the concrete, still for a long time. Either I was about to die there, or they'd get tired of the game and leave.

Eventually, the cheers died down, and I heard the low rumbling of motorcycle engines before glass stopped flying at me altogether.

"Welcome to the hood," I vaguely remember hearing Heist congratulating calmly before I passed out.

death is easy

"闲梦江南梅熟日·夜船吹笛雨潇潇·人语驿边桥"
—皇甫松《梦江南》

Idalia

Surprisingly, I had a restful night for the first time since I quit taking melatonin pills. I yawned, leisurely waking up at nine. Interesting—maybe I needed to fight with people more, just casually drain out energy.

Last night, I got mad over nothing. I laughed as I brushed out my tangled hair, sitting at the vanity in the wrinkly white slip and dark blue cardigan I fell asleep in. I had forgotten that was only last night; it felt like ages. He had sex—so what? If I'm being honest with myself, I liked how experienced he was. Kinda hard to be experienced without the ... experience, don't you think? Not to mention it was four years ago. *He's not mine; he's his own being. As I am my own being,* I thought cheerfully.

I felt a surge of wetness down my legs and heard a knock at the door as I ran to the bathroom, calling out, "Give me a second!" Oh, *oh*, I realized as I saw red. That explained it. The flying emotions and the violent cramp that woke me up briefly at six. I cleaned myself up and then dashed to the door before whoever was on the other side left. I opened the door, a broad smile reaching my eyes. "Morning!"

Tashi observed for a second, trying to decide how to respond: he probably envisioned me greeting him with every other mood ... except cheerfulness. "Sleep well?"

"Very. Come in," I gestured.

"Are you ... still mad? I'm still in trouble for failing to invent a time machine, yeah?"

He described my light laughter as floating across the room like a Chopin concerto, and I liked that. He was forgiven. Yes, definitely for failing to invent a time machine. I would have liked one. The Victorian Era and the Antebellum South always intrigued me.

"Hey, about last night. I'm sorry. I ... I don't know where the outburst came from. I guess ..." I stopped, feeling ridiculous.

"No worries. Come on, let's go."

I told Tashi to wait while I changed, but he looked me up and down, wondering why I needed to. Blast that voice who told me his look had an effect on me. It did not. I was not fazed, at all.

"Because I am a mess," I explained, wondering why the obvious needed an explanation.

"You? You and your camellia beauty that could stop me in my tracks had I climbed across a desert for seven days and there was a well behind you?"

I rolled my eyes, thinking that was honestly more creative than any other compliment I'd heard. This was no prosaic accountant standing in my room. This was no ruthless investment banker standing in front of me. This man had *lived*, I could tell, and to undermine my jealousy would be lying to myself.

"Come on, it was a literary masterpiece, give me some credit," he protested when I didn't respond. What was I supposed to respond with? Doey-eyed admiration? I could do better than that.

"Yeah? You're dead by day three," I dismissed. "Where are we going?"

"Mystery."

"Hiking?"

"Why would I keep that a mystery?"

"Sahara Desert?"

"Close," he winked.

"You've got to stop doing that to me," I said.

"What?"

"Stopping my heart without a warning."

His smile reached his eyes as I struggled to survive under the heat. I bet I was the only one in that entire climate struggling.

* * *

I heard the piercing screams of excited kids playing beneath the mountains before I saw a red brick schoolhouse next to a café. Pine trees peered over the back of the schoolhouse, framing a picture of pure ecstasy.

As we started walking toward the kids, Tashi began explaining the tie between the orphanage and the tea shop, or tea café. The physical shop didn't have a sign or anything that indicated its name. It didn't need to search for customers; customers were constantly looking for it. All its revenue either went toward overhead costs or the needs of the orphanage.

I saw the kids playing a game of "Duck, Duck, Goose," except with a red bandanna instead of smacking people on the head. Personally, I thought it was a better version of the game. Some of the boys, bored of the pace, started playing what I will refer to as "I Hit You on the Head and You're Supposed to Duck Except You Didn't so I Hit Again." I stood in utter awe, seeing my vision executed before my eyes. I *had* to meet this owner.

Tashi described Jiangnan, the founder, to me as one of the most tenacious people he'd ever had the honor to know. During the Great Wenchuan Earthquake in '08, nearly seventy thousand people from her home province were killed. He promised I'd get to meet her; he had a feeling I'd absolutely adore her. *Without a doubt*, I thought, my hand gently sweeping dirt off two names engraved on the bench out front.

The ambiance of that place was unlike any other. This wasn't commercial; it was cultural. With a light, open interior design, a perfect juxtaposition of modern minimalism coincided with traditional Chinese elements. The wall of tea displayed in the background, the ink paintings of terraneous skylines and silky waterfalls, and a Guzheng performer greeted visitors upon stepping inside. Dressed in Tang dynasty costume, her balance between sophistication and warmth never tipped over. She glanced up as we walked in, smiling faintly before looking back down at her music sheet. How graceful her fingers glided across the strings. She was royalty itself, an empress who time traveled into the wrong era. It was in the knowing expression and her magnanimous essence, the laugh lines around her eyes and the wrinkles on her hands. Laugh lines are glorious, a testament that she found the strength to keep on laughing through her long life. Music soared like magic under her wings.

To the right, behind the performer, was a little room with glass walls. A class was going on: a teacher stood at the front showing a presentation of different tea pots as students took notes.

"The students seem touristy," I wondered.

"They offer classes a few times per week during peak travel season," Tashi answered as we sat down at the bar in the back. This bar served both tea and cocktails, a concept that expressed how tea can also be a performance. He gestured at the menu to ask if I had decided.

I shook my head and shrugged. "Recommendations?"

"Mengshan is a tea you *cannot* miss out on."

"Why?"

"It's a type of green tea produced right here in the mountains of Sichuan; its history spans across the last two thousand years. There are ... seven? I think seven categories of Mengshan tea. I don't know the specifics or how to differentiate them, but in general, geography is critical to tea's production. Sichuan has exactly what Mengshan needs to grow well."

"Sold. I'll get that," I approved.

"Well that was easy. I should sell you premium water from a McDonald's sink or something."

"What was it you were saying about the tea classes?"

"Huh? Oh, classes," he glanced up at the waiter whose name tag read Alex. "Two sets of Mengshan tea please, thank you."

Tashi looked back to me. "Classes. The amount of knowledge and particularity that goes into tea culture is insane. The type and categories, where it's produced, where it originates, the right temperature of the water for each type, the tea pot that pairs best with each type, the temperament, the mood or state of mind you can train yourself to be in as you sip on it, every aspect involves an erudition to it."

"Can we please take one?" My excitement clouded over logistics, as it often does. My departure to Inner Mongolia was twenty-four hours out.

"Next time you're here," he promised as Jiangnan came out from the office inside.

I could tell this was Jiangnan from the way she strode across the room, as if she owned the place. She did.

"Tashi," she exclaimed warmly from across the bar, walking over to give him a hug. "And this is …?" she gestured toward me.

"I'm Yu Xiao, pleasure to meet you. If you have time, please, sit for a while," I got up, pulling out the chair beside her. Because I only used this name with my parents, it had special meaning I knew Jiangnan would understand. I was not disappointed.

"Yu Xiao, is that from a poem?" Jiangnan brightened up even more radiantly.

I nodded, smiling. When I wrote the two characters out on a napkin, she gasped, reciting the right poem. Of course she would be the one to know. I gave her a thumbs up. "This place is full of stories—I can almost sense it. What's the story behind the orphanage?"

In an evanescent moment, a wave of pain shot across Jiangnan's face as her mind flashed back to many years ago.

* * *

Debris. Ruins. Wasteland. Seventy thousand dead people.
It would've been facile to simply lie there in peace. To consign to the menacing darkness. The thunderous noise from the previous BANG drowned out the sensitivity in my ears, and it was quieter than it had been in years.
My eyelids drooped.
My breathing became heavy.
When was the last time I had a good night's rest? Approximately ten years ago, before my son was born.
My son!
My eyelids fluttered open amidst the dust, and I found my will to climb out. I churned my ears toward the pandemonium, and began crawling, one hand, one knee at a time. When I got to a position where I could stick a free hand out toward the light, I began to scream.
"Help!" I called hoarsely.
An eternity later, three soldiers tugged me out of the debris. My body aquiver with the pleasure of seeing light again, I immediately questioned them about my children.
"We need to send you to the hospital first," a soldier answered, concern in his voice.
I nodded a thank you, but no thank you. Limping away from the stretcher, I anxiously stopped anyone passing by.
No one knew where my little girl was. No one had heard about my son.
"Muyun, Mujin!" After each time I gulped a mouthful of water, I would call their names out again. For a second, I thought I heard an echo; quickly realizing it wasn't my voice, I turned and saw my husband, his hand cupped, croaking out the two names that meant more to us than life itself.
We limped to each other. He barely had time to wipe away my tears before I pointed to the right and steered him toward

that direction.

"You search over there, I'll go that way. When it gets dark, we meet back here." I marked our ground with a deep line in the dirt.

The moon switched out the sun, but it still wouldn't switch out my excruciating anxiety. Meeting my husband, both of us not having found a sliver of information or hope, I screamed at the unbothered moon.

Why? Would that my life could be exchanged for theirs.

One sleepless night later, a soldier ran up to us at the temporary housing area, asking if we were Muyun and Mujin's parents.

"They're alive?" I wailed.

"I ... uh, follow me." The soldier didn't look me in the eye. I exchanged a glance with my husband.

And we sprinted behind him.

At the almost-gravesite of our children, the rescuers explained what was going on. Buried under a block of concrete on opposite sides, my angels were barely breathing. They couldn't lift the entire block because the whole structure would crumple if they tried. The hole they dug would cave in immediately. Both would die.

"Quick, make a decision!" a rescuer shouted.

Make a decision? A decision? Between my children? Would that the earth could swallow me whole.

I couldn't breathe, much less talk.

"Quick!" people shouted at us.

I bent down on my knees. "Muyun? Mujin?"

"Mommy." I heard Mujin's weak voice.

"Yes? I'm here; I'll never leave you. We'll get you out. Don't worry." I had to stay strong; I didn't know where I found the courage to think it would be okay.

"I heard them. Save ... save my sister."
God. Why? If You exist, why is this happening to my innocent children? Take my life. Switch me out.
Why?
God. If You don't exist, the devil surely does. Take my husband's and mine. Two for two.
As I sobbed to the point of collapsing, the rescuers started tipping the concrete over to our son's side. Just as they started, my husband dived in. Head first. I think ... he was trying to shelter Mujin's body with his own.
They died upon impact.
Be careful what you wish for.

* * *

"Jiangnan?" I reiterated carefully.
"I'm sorry. I remembered something—I have to go." She got up.
I smiled warmly. I didn't know if that was what made her sit back down for the next few hours as we sipped tea and observed the children at play, relaying her story.
"I lost my husband and son in an earthquake. The one person keeping me from suicide was my daughter—she needed me, I'd tell myself every day."
Outside the window, one girl started climbing up a tree, swift as a monkey. A lazy *sirimiri* drizzled on this laughing monkey.
"For weeks, I numbed myself to the pain. Silence ate me alive. Can you imagine? Going from a home filled with laughter, always chaotic in the mornings, everyone rushing to get somewhere, children fighting all the time, my husband humming as we made dinner together, to silence? I

couldn't even bring myself to comfort my daughter, to be a valid mom." Jiangnan sighed, pouring out more tea and taking a slow sip.

I wasn't drawing enough air; I stood in my own water-less, oxygen-less atmosphere, unable to produce enough tears to distract my pain. Did I even have a right to grieve? This was not my story.

Agony engulfing her senses, Jiangnan went days without eating. Muyun begged her to talk, to do anything but sit in Mujin's room, smelling his clothes, and all she could manage was to get up and cook something for her. At one point, her body caved in. She caught a fever that escalated throughout the night. Nurses cooled it down with an IV drip, but when she recovered, the amount of desperation and death she saw gnawed at her.

"I can't tell you the number of times I thought about joining my husband and son. I saw their faces vividly as heaven's gates opened for me. Death would be so easy; it's living that's the hardest."

"Death is easy; living is hard," I repeated.

"In my time at the hospital, I met a boy who reminded me of my son. Intelligent eyes and what I assumed would've been quick-witted humor, had he been in the mood for humor. I don't know, something about his essence gave me the idea," she described, her eyes crinkling at the corners. "He was only eight, and the earthquake made an orphan out of him. He never knew his mother, and his father was a builder. Ironically, the construction his father built was what … what trapped him."

I nodded, hurting for the boy in her story. The boy who probably didn't need me to hurt for him, as he was a million times more tenacious than I was.

"I took him home with me. The government had policies for victims of the earthquake, yet with that much destruction, innocent people were bound to slip through the social net," Jiangnan said, exasperated. "The more I researched this issue, the angrier I became. I heard local news about human traffickers dressing up as social workers to exploit lost kids. That's what spurred my idea."

Alex came by with a pad, asking Jiangnan a question about an invoice statement. After apologizing, he said he didn't know whether they had to send the statement out that day or not. I hadn't noticed that in my conversation with Jiangnan, the sky had already started turning dark.

Jiangnan glanced through the paperwork quickly, looking up at Alex. "Send it out today." Looking back into my eyes, she concluded, "Death is the easy way out, but we take the harder one when we realize what it is we stay alive for."

Phenomenal. Pure serendipity ushers forth the best inspiration. In somber silence, Tashi and I drove home. We decided on long distance, but I hated goodbyes more than anything in the world.

i was too late

Arno

Flash back

"Whatever you're doing, get out of it," Mr. Raleigh, my world history teacher, pulled me aside one day to tell me.

I frowned, not saying anything. Who did he think he was? This was my life. Sure, I'd been a good student before, I liked his class, we had some friendly conversations, but there were limits to how much a teacher could help me. The streets were where brotherhood was at. We were family.

Everyone called me Young Money in those days. Being Young Money helped me take care of my dad, who would've been decaying by the minute if I wasn't. They told me that the crack we sold earned us $30,000 a month. Divided twelve ways—I got to take home $2,500 a month and all I had to do was grab the crack from the dealer near where I used to work. And not get caught. If they didn't see my face, they couldn't identify me. We spent the rest of the time high, partying, picking up girls, something stupid, or a combination of all four.

"And look me in the eye," Mr. Raleigh added sternly.

I did. The worry in them scared me. I quickly looked away.

"I won't pretend to understand what's going on in your life, but the effect it's having on you, I can see it. And I'm not about to pretend it's not concerning me. What are your plans for the future?"

Future? I huffed out some air through my nose, a semblance of a sarcastic laugh. My future was gone the minute my mom left us. The divorce cost her my college savings.

"Um, my next class is in a minute," I finally replied, packing up to go.

"You skip school three days out of five on average, yet your grades in my class never drop. Either you still care or you're a genius."

Or I cheat through the tests. I continued walking away.

"What is it? Drugs? The hood? What are you doing?" Mr. Raleigh demanded.

That stopped me. I turned around.

"Why do you care?" My tone was rude; so pardon me for giving off the impression that I gave a shit. I did not. "If college is what you're talking about, I got rid of that idea a long time ago. I'm not going to college."

"Why not? You have it in you. You're smart. You're curious," Mr. Raleigh encouraged.

"You really want me to say it? I might have the brains but I don't have the money."

"We can get you scholarships; there are lots of ways you can get loans. I will help you with this. If money is what you're worried about, I'll take care of it. We'll get you to college."

"No thank you," I replied coldly, taking a few more steps toward the door. I needed him to leave me alone. To stop caring about me. Heaven knows everyone else did a long time ago.

"You're better than whatever they're making you do." Every word he was saying was like a knife stabbing me where it actually hurt. I *used to* have goals. They didn't matter anymore.

"No, I'm not," I finished, really turning my back on him to walk away.

"I'm telling you—get out. Do something useful with your life. If they won't let you get out, move somewhere else. Start over. I'll buy you a ticket."

How many times have I wanted to do just that? Well, I can't, sir. Whether I go home to feed my dinosaur or I head to India to make rotis is beyond your business.

"I said, no thank you."

That didn't deter him. "We can get help for your dad if that's what's stopping you."

"From who? The state? Authorities? You act as if I haven't tried everything else before. You don't get it! Stop trying to fucking care!" I finally screamed with my back still turned to him, running out of that classroom.

The last thing I heard was him screaming down the hallway, "Did you forget about Yale?"

How could I forget? Yale was everything I wanted, everything I had been working toward before I transferred. The books I read, the sports I played, the videos I filmed. I wanted to study film and media.

Instead, I dropped out of school that very day.

* * *

I did go back. Eventually. Many years later, after I was accepted into college, I wanted to tell him I never would've made it if he didn't believe in me. Jim, that was his name. Dad had already passed away. Mom transferred me everything she had in her account before she got married to some rich Goldman Sachs banker. Might've been more had she not have to fight a legal battle to shorten my sentence. As much as I hated what she did to us, the money gave me a new start.

I walked into my old high school, asking the Hispanic woman at the front desk for Jim Raleigh. Mr. Raleigh. She was quite the attractive type; I wondered how she ended up as an inner-city high school administrator.

"He's not ... here any ... more," she stammered.

"He's not here anymore? Well do you have his contact information?" I asked, my heart sinking. That meant I had to track him down.

"He's not here as in he passed away," she revealed.

"What ... He ... Wait, how? He was so young ..." I couldn't believe my ears. He had to be around forty when I was here—the oldest he could be right now was fifty.

"Cancer, stage four," she replied. "I'm sorry."

"When was this?" I asked.

"He passed away a year ago. It was too late for any revolutionary type of treatment. He taught for as long as he could—it's what made him happy. We all miss him very much."

I remember thinking, *No. No no no no no no no. It's not true. It can't be true. He was a kind man, the kindest man I've ever had the honor to know. Heaven didn't need another angel. I needed an angel.*

Kangbashi

Idalia

I joined my family after I met Jiangnan. If Sichuan satisfied my longing for a sip of authentic minority culture, Inner Mongolia opened my eyes to something even greater: the reality hidden behind tourist hot spots. I will forever be indebted to my parents for teaching us that traveling was not about Instagram posts, but the understanding of lifestyles and mindsets different than our own. It formed the foundation to all my travels in the future: observe and learn. Respect the culture, and try as hard as you can to take your colored lenses off.

Stepping into Ordos Kangbashi, we were immediately greeted by signs that said "the most famous tourist city." A quick glance around the area had me wondering where all the tourists were. Its peaceful quiet juxtaposed its sophisticated urban development, making me all the more curious.

In Xi'an, especially at night when we walked through the city wall brimming with night life, I could not tell you what we went there to do because all I saw was a sea of people everywhere I turned.

In most major cities like Shanghai, Beijing, Chongqing, Tianjin, Guangzhou, Shenzhen, oceans of people swimming between your location and your destination were more likely than not.

In Ordos, there was either a party I was not invited to or aliens had abducted everyone overnight. The art museum was literally in the shape of what looked to me like a spaceship. Wrapped in polished metal louvers, it was both windowless and menacing. Inside, the heights of the walls were disproportionate, holes in the walls were interlaced with staircases, and through an opening in the ceiling, light cascaded on different surfaces in organic rays that created beautiful stages for shadow to play. Staring at this art museum, if some small green humanoid with antennas were to walk out, I'd shrug like they were meant to be there—I was invading *their* spaceship. I could not figure out why this promising, clean, futuristic city steaming with investment had no bustling sense of life to it.

Situated right next to the museum was a library designed to look like a stack of books. Creative. If they asked me, I would've suggested something less predictable, like, I don't know, a spaceship. They deserved credit for the disarray of the stack of books, though. Architects spent a tremendous amount of time getting it to look unaligned.

The city square was designed to replicate a Mongolian chess piece surrounded by golden statues. The carnival in the middle of it had very few people, which meant very few lines, which meant more rides to ride and more money to spend! For our parents. Zion, Legend, and I had a fabulous time. However, it wasn't for long before we needed to check in at a hotel. This was a disaster from the very start.

Security wasn't heavy as we were getting into Inner Mongolia, but checking in at the hotel was a whole different monster to tackle. Because our parents, at the time, had green cards and a Chinese passport, the hotel asked for their Chinese resident identity card. My parents patiently explained that they'd lived in the US for almost a decade, and the identity card was long lost, might even be expired—they never thought they'd need it. The front desk politely said she needed to talk to her manager. The manager came out, and sternly asked why they had green cards while their children have US passports, and since they walked around with a Chinese passport, why they didn't have their resident identity card?

Then came the real questioning. Where are you from? What are you doing here? How long are you staying? When are you going back to America?—it all felt like an invasion of privacy to me. Was security really the reason?

"It's nearly impossible for a foreigner to get a Chinese passport, so we thought if we kept the Chinese citizenship and lived in America with a green card, we'd have our country to come back to when our children are older," my dad explained as calmly as he could manage.

"I'm sorry, but we need that resident ID if you're not technically considered a foreigner. It's against policy to let you in for legal reasons. *My* boss will punish me for it," the manager empathized.

We'd never been turned away from a hotel before—it was a little embarrassing. Truly. We searched up a smaller motel next, hoping that their protocol was less rigid. To our great relief, this one didn't ask too many questions. We were able to check in to our rooms smoothly. As soon as I settled down, two knocks at the door had us moving again.

"Pack up your bags, they're kicking us out," my dad instructed.

I could only laugh, what else was there to do? "Why?" Did I really need to ask that question? "What are we going to do? Go back to grandma's house?"

"Let me call a friend first. I'm not sure if he's here, but I know he has business in the area. Third time's the charm. We'll see if he has connections," my dad answered.

Dad's childhood friend came through—one of his managers, Ganzorig, personally came and drove us to a hotel they had connections with. They haggled, they begged, they brought up past dealings, but at the end of the day ...

"Will you please make an exception for me? You trust me, these are my close friends." Ganzorig motioned to us, ushering forth his charisma. "If you don't let them in, they might have to sleep on the streets tonight."

"No one's stopping you from taking them home," the manager suggested, trying to be helpful.

"My house is too small for five people—we only have one spare couch."

"Last time we made an exception for a similar situation we were fined by regulators—trust me, I want to," sympathized this manager.

Ganzorig tried another method. "Their youngest kid is only six, they wouldn't dare to do anything out of line. And look—their daughter is going to college after this vacation. They're *good* people."

"I believe so, I really do. But my power is limited, please understand."

To make it worse, it started pouring rain. Lightning flashing, thunder echoing, we ran to Ganzorig's car soaking wet.

We sincerely thanked Ganzorig—he really tried, but immediately we started to look for the first flight out of Inner Mongolia.

"I can't let you guys go like this. My boss would kill me for being such an incapable host," Ganzorig started.

"No, no, it's really our fault. We came unprepared," my mom assured him.

Ganzorig suddenly looked as if he'd revolutionized the Industrial Revolution. "Let's try one more method: the police station."

That sent shivers up my spine; I gave Legend a look saying "we're really about to head to jail for this." Ganzorig told us the police have the right to issue a statement declaring that we were genuinely here for vacation.

The cop was generous: after questioning us, filling out paperwork, issuing the statement, he personally drove with us to another hotel to assuage the manager and explain the situation. That was cause for celebration, to say the least.

At midnight, after checking in, we set out to find food. In the car, I stood on top of the center console, sticking my body through the sunroof. Shouting with my hands in the air into the echoing city with few cars in the deserted streets, blasting music with no fear of disrupting anyone, I loved Inner Mongolia all the more. Watching the city where stars shone in full force in a night sky with no pollution, as much as I wanted to keep this magic to myself, I realized that any city needed people to stay alive.

A coal-mining boom early on led the local government to throw money into urban development (hundreds of millions of dollars). When it didn't work out as planned, developers—scaling back their ambitions in creating an epicenter of culture and a financial hub—kept trying to make it known for its architectural projects, residential towers, and state of the art venues. Even still, deadlines weren't being met, loans weren't being paid, investors were pulling out, and high property taxes kept people from moving to Ordos. The city remains developing, the framed picture of a housing bubble burst.

"Is it only the high taxes? What else prevents people from moving in?" Legend asked Ganzorig.

"Do you understand the fundamental difference between the real estate development cycle in China versus the US?"

"All I know is rich people buy property like they buy groceries for investment, so much of their property is empty."

"That's one factor, but even with the middle class, something you'd want to take note of is that selling of apartment units don't start until around eighty, eighty-five percent of the construction is finished. Plus, it's standard for the buyer in China to furnish the interior themselves. That takes at least a year after the purchase, and maybe another year to ventilate the units. This makes selling and settling in Ordos even slower."

"Ordos is beautiful—it's only a matter of time before people recognize it," Legend remarked.

I later found the secret to reversing its fate was in education: moving the best schools into the city would lure parents to occupy the properties.

da-dum-da-dum-da-dum

Tashi

The news of my father hit me like a meteorite.

I had been in Vietnam negotiating with a local supplier when I got the call from my mother.

"You need to come back—now," I remembered her demanding.

"I'll be back in a week."

"No, drop everything."

"What? Why? I just got out of a meeting with …"

"It doesn't matter anymore!" she interrupted, unlike her usual self.

I took the hint to shut up.

She went on. "Your father—he …"

The line went silent while she collected herself. Even uttering words was onerous for her; I waited, and nothing else came.

"What happened?" I finally asked.

"He's in the emergency room."

I flew back from Ho Chi Minh in the beat of a drum. I felt like each second passing by was a drum beat. *Da-dum-da-dum-da-dum.* The flight attendants walked around slower than pregnant turtles, greeting every passenger, checking each bag, demonstrating every rule. Seriously, make these flight attendants run a race with a loggerhead in the middle of laying her eggs, and the loggerhead would still win.

I want to murder one of them. I'll get up and fly the plane myself for goodness' sake. We get it. Wear your seat belt. Wear your oxygen mask when it pops out. Exit when everyone else exits. Now shut the fuck up so I can go home.

Every millisecond was an eternity; ten million, eight hundred thousand eternities later, I arrived. All I could think about in the cab from the airport to the hospital was all the times I forgot what filial piety was. All the times I shouted at my dad for stupid things, like disagreeing on a supplier, hiring a new employee, making me come back to run the family business.

I remembered all the good times like it was yesterday—because they were so few and far in between. I was sent away in high school; during those four years, the only conversations I had with my father were about money. *How much do you need? I need this much. Okay.* That was it.

All I wanted was for my father to be alive when I arrived. Once there, I charged into the hospital, spotting my mother petrified in front of the emergency room.

"What's the situation?" I panicked, grasping her shoulders tightly.

"Intracerebral brain hemorrhage," my mother stuttered.

"What does that mean?"

She shook her head, staring blankly at the red emergency sign.

The doctor explained my father's case was a ruptured aneurysm—an enlarged artery—which caused bleeding in the brain. He proceeded to throw out a bunch of words that I could not comprehend, words like amyloid angiopathy and hematoma that had ratios of eight to one in terms of syllable to word.

I stepped closer, menacingly. "Just tell me how likely it is he'll survive."

"Greater than two thirds chance of survival, but only twenty percent of those who do survive will gain functional independence."

Those words I understood. A thirteen percent chance he'd be normal.

The craniotomy was "successful"—at least, heartbeat-wise.

* * *

They might as well have just killed me, such was the blow of the 66,146.22 RMB bill that came afterwards, excluding the nights my father spent in the ICU. The business had already taken out a massive loan to start up in Vietnam. I'd have to kill to pay it back—investors in Vietnam had already started pulling out as soon as they heard the news of my father's stroke.

It wasn't like me to panic, so I did what I could. I shuttered operations in Vietnam; I canceled all supplier bids. Out of the fifty employees on my payroll, I sent fifteen of them home. I cleared out their wages in cash right before they left.

A few days later, my phone rang. It was an unknown number, but the woman identified herself as the wife of one of my father's longtime associates, Zhu Yongchang.

"How much is your father's medical bill?" the woman began.

I wondered where she got the news. It was probably through the mouth of one of the employees I sent back to the countryside.

"Why?"

"I want to help you—your father knows my husband well."

I declined telling the number to this woman, Suo Xiu. I could not pinpoint what she was up to.

"32,000 RMB," Suo Xiu stated.

That caught my attention. "What?"

"I will give you 32,000 for a young girl between fifteen and twenty-five, someone who has no family to return to."

"You think I'm desperate enough to stoop that low?" I fumed.

"Consider it. It's not wrong if I treat her well, and if you think about it, why would I abuse the mother of a grandson that doesn't exist yet? I will only want her to be as healthy and happy as possible so she can bear a child," Xiu proposed calmly.

I hung up on her. *Unbelievable.*

on not belonging

Idalia

College—ever after.

If only that were the case.

I looked at the ebb and flow of people walking in and out of class, and it wasn't hard to imagine my life from now to fifty: three sides of a cubicle and a spreadsheet every day, eight hours a day for years. I'd get promoted eventually, and my days would be meetings meetings meetings. More meetings. Decisions. Mortgages. Children. Saving up for their college. The predictability terrorized me.

It was even more scary to think that the conversations around this circle would still be NFL, stocks and bonds, where to eat, and how to make more money ten years from now.

I could not say I didn't care, because I did. I could not say I didn't need the money, because I did need it. I could not say that the chimeras of stocks and bonds were useless, because they weren't. You simply do not call the engine that powers the biggest economy in the world useless. They were useful, very much so. I just couldn't get myself to care.

Because I couldn't care, I forced myself to pretend.

I signed up for Robinhood when the stock trading and investment app—aka the people's broker—went controversially public. I bought ten whole dollars of GameStop. I traded my AMC stocks. I was bored. I got the big concepts down, I did. I just didn't know how to apply them. Accounting was the most straightforward thing ever, theoretically—so why did I suck?

I didn't mind finance because, if anything, it taught me how to put a number on my ideas, which was useful everywhere.

I was always so busy pretending that it ultimately backfired, and I never had enough time to do anything right. My relationship included.

Who am I?

* * *

pg. 17

when i stand in Your presence
all noise dies down

Lord i need You to speak to me, <u>now</u>
why do i suck at Everything?
even when i try so hard to not
suck

what do i do

Jesus i honestly
am done
i honestly
cannot
deal with myself
any longer

You
deal with me
i'll surrender everything
i don't have anything

You
fix me
i'll give You everything
which is nothing

but
when i'm at this breaking point
that's where You want me to be
right?

when i don't have any pride left
when i'm so far into hopeless i've forgotten
    who i worship
You tell me,

Because I AM worthy
so you are
for you are
daughter of the Highest King

* * *

pg. 18

i feel like i've never really belonged anywhere ...
and i know i have a home in the states
a home in China
because home is where family is and
i know, i've felt unbelievable, overwhelming
connection with some of the most amazing people
deep, splendid human interaction i love and crave
late night talks till daybreak and
early morning coffee and
all-nighters at the library and
i genuinely love group work because when
synergy happens
we get phenomenal work done but
i just
don't
really
belong
anywhere.
i cannot be bound to one place
live in one way
i cannot die without a legacy and
what even is a legacy
the very thought is so stupid
why does it matter how they remember you when
you don't have time to see for yourself when
you don't have time to edit their
    perception when

you want to do something both kind and great and
i always sound so contradictory but i swear it's
collectively exhaustive like
the idea is to work toward something more than
    yourself and
the other idea is to leave a legacy for yourself
and
it seems mutually exclusive but
no
i will not die without a legacy
i will not die before i do something
    overwhelmingly kind
the world is where i belong and
heaven after that
so
if adventures meant seeing the world,
    doing something for it and
home meant being with you—
i can have both ...
can't i?

i promise

Tashi

Agonizing days of work were followed by tormenting nights of insomnia.

We were so far in debt that I glanced at the homeless on my way driving my father to the hospital for a check-up, envying them for being wealthier than us. They weren't tens of thousands of RMB in debt. I'd rather start again at zero than negative.

It was so tense at home that it was far more torturous to be there than working in the office. My father carved a solid scowl into his face; my mother did everything humanly possible to please him, yet all he wanted was to be able to do something by himself.

My father lost all function in the entire right side of his brain, so he couldn't move the left side of his body. One day, he was determined to learn how to walk. My mother went ecstatic, joyously jumping for excitement at seeing his will to live again. He was convinced that as long as the right side of his body was strong enough, it'd force the left side to cooperate. We did not break it to him that the doctor already deemed recovery of the right brain "nearly impossible."

Every day after dinner, the whole family exercised with him, cheering him on. Leg raises, three sets of ten each. Colorful dumbbells, my mother bought a whole set, despite my father only being able to use one out of the twelve. For a while, the atmosphere seemed to creep into a happier territory. My mother was deceived, or she let herself be deceived. I caught her humming again as she dusted off shelves.

Two months into working out, father vehemently decided he would try to walk on his cane. By himself. Nothing we said could stop him; he only became angrier with our continued objections.

One try. Two tries. After trying thirty times, we were shocked to discover he had stood up on his right leg, one hand on the cane, the other on the wall. He smiled with half his face. We smiled with him. The next second we both lunged to catch him as he fell.

He wanted to try again. What else could we do but cheer him on?

Forty-three attempts later, my mother reached out to stop him. He grunted, shoving her back.

She pinned him down. "You will overexert yourself. Stop!"

Then, the unthinkable happened. My father threw his cane at her. Luckily, with his unbalanced hand-eye coordination, he missed. But it was the first time in his life he had tried something even remotely close.

* * *

That night, Suo Xiu called me again using a different phone number.

"Thirty-five thousand," she proposed without a hello.

"Hear me out. The older employees who worked for you for decades must already be isolating her—she is the only one you kept that is new. You will have to end up firing her anyways, and she'll have nowhere to go. She doesn't know the language, she doesn't have a residence permit, she doesn't know how to find a new job. She doesn't have a home to go back to. Then *you* would be a murderer, much worse than handing her to *me*, who will treat her better than a queen; you're better off saving your own indebted ass."

Illegal immigration was a problem everywhere—everywhere from the EU with its refugees, to America with its stupid wall, to here in Asia. It was different in China because each location had its own residence permit (*hukou*); a citizen of China could be deemed a foreigner in their own country because the hukou system classifies all citizens by type: rural and urban, local or non-local. The urban designation gives certain rights to its possessors—social services such as housing, employment, education and health care—unavailable to those with an agricultural hukou. The local designation of an agricultural hukou gives access to the locality's services and privileges, such as compensation for a home the government tears down to upgrade the infrastructure.

With Dolkar's situation, she didn't have a hukou anywhere; she didn't have the papers to legally reside or work anywhere. I hired a tea merchant Jiangnan introduced me to who regularly does business across Myanmar and China to drive her in as a visiting relative; with his reputation, it wasn't painstakingly difficult to finesse her across the border.

Who was telling this woman all of this though? Most importantly, how did *they* know? I wondered if someone internal had ratted us out. No one came to mind. How far did this woman's tentacles reach?

"The older employees love Dolkar. Thank you." I hung up.

Truth be told, the other employees did not like Dolkar at all. But it wasn't until later that I realized Suo Xiu had pointed out someone specific this time.

Who was telling her all of this?

* * *

Days turned into nights, and nights turned into days. I didn't want to face my family, so I worked after hours and went home only to sleep.

One evening, I came home earlier than usual. As I walked into the kitchen, I saw the silhouette of my mother, her head in her hands. Tiptoeing into the dark living room, lit by a single yellow lamp, I heard her weeping quietly, trying to suck her ruptured breaths back in. Each trial made the weeping worse. This woman never wept. I didn't know what to do.

Eventually, I came around to sitting next to her, putting one hand on her shoulder. *When had it become this bony?*

As she lifted her head, the bruise on the side of her face became apparent to me. It was an ugly spreading purple with yellow blotches.

"Mother! Your face! What happened?"

"It's nothing, really," she consoled me.

I took a few minutes to smother my red hot fury. Anger doesn't solve problems.

"He did this to you?" I confronted.

She went silent. I didn't have to ask again. I coerced myself to stop wondering if it would've been more peaceful had the surgery been unsuccessful.

* * *

The third time an unknown number reached my phone, I knew exactly who it was. I took a deep breath, once and for all, and hit the red button. She called three more times. I turned off my phone.

Three days later, she arrived in person. She came bearing gifts.

"Fish oil and omegas, for your husband. Only the best. I imported them! He'll be walking in days," she smiled brightly at my mother, handing her the packages.

I wanted to shut her out, but what could I do? I came home to her already sitting in the living room, tea in her hands. The bruise on my mother's face was as apparent as daylight. I wanted to strangle this woman.

"A word with your son? I have a business proposition," Suo Xiu said.

"Of course, he's all yours!" my mother exclaimed. I wished she knew she was feeding me to a Luna wolf; I wished she could stop temptation like all the times she spanked me with stinging nettles when I was young. They say temptation beholds itself resplendently, that it doesn't start off with a feeling of sin but with an illusion that you're doing a great deed, that you're making the right choice.

The right choice, yes.

As we walked outside, out of earshot of my mother, Suo Xiu began with pleasantries instead of a number. I was in no mood for useless chatter with her.

"I can see you don't want to talk to me. Once and for all, 40,000 RMB," she enunciated the number. "Look at me. Do I look like someone low enough to stick around abusing innocent girls? I just want my husband's bloodline to be carried on, that's all. My son works at the police station; all the village girls are scared of him, and he's getting old. I've heard Dolkar is a beauty, that's why I came all the way here."

"How does this make me any less of a human trafficker?" I questioned.

"Why of course this is different! Why would the thought enter your mind?" Suo Xiu exclaimed. "Because you and I are different. I want to help you out, so it's like I'm hiring her from you—she will be paid with housing, food, and clothing. There's incentive for me to treat her well, as you know the only reason I'm here is because I want a grandson. Rest assured—I will be the one serving *her*, not the other way around."

"We have to ask what she wants," I finally decided.

* * *

I felt like the reincarnation of the devil as I pulled Dolkar aside from the dining area.

Suo Xiu was right; she was a beauty. I'd never noticed before. Dolkar wiped her hands off on her apron, looking up at me inquisitively in her long, lush eyelashes and those knowing brown eyes. I explained my father's situation to her; I emphasized the fact that I could no longer afford to have her there.

"I know you'd never go back home, and if I fire you out of the blue, you'll have nowhere to go without a residence permit, so I found you a new job. The work is similar, and the living conditions are even better. It will be a safe and secure place for you to live." I kept repeating *this is for the best* under my breath until I even started believing myself. Maybe this *was* for the best. *What I cannot provide for her, Suo Xiu will.*

I saw her look back down, blushing.

"Would you rather work there or go back to Myanmar?" I connived.

"Work," Dolkar said simply.

"I'll arrange it for you—I promise you'll be in good hands."

"But ..." she stammered.

"What's up?" I turned back around.

"Will I be able to visit Eindra?"

For a second, I was confused, and then I realized she was asking if she'd be able to see her mother again. "Of course. To tell you the truth, it will be a bit far, so maybe not very often. But for the holidays, I will personally call Suo Xiu to arrange it for you."

I made a mental note to save Suo Xiu's latest number.

you'll be safe

Dolkar

I woke up in a van driving on mountain roads, ones much like the road I came to the Norzins' on. I tried to remember what happened before I got here. Escapades were coming to me in flashing images now, and I tried my best to think through what happened.

I remembered the news of Mr. Norzin being sent to the hospital, how fear spread like wildfire around the homestay for months on end. We feared for our jobs.

I remembered being pulled aside by Tashi—how madly I was blushing when he spoke to me directly. He gently explained the situation, that he couldn't afford to employ or house me anymore, but promised that where I was going to would be safe; "secure" was another word he used. He told me they'd pay me the same wage, that I'd have a place to stay and food to eat.

I remembered packing up what little I had, looking back one last time at this boy whose smile drew out the gods.

I remembered losing my mother. Before I met her, I couldn't comprehend the hole I felt in my chest. When Eindra and I separated for the second time, I saw my mother-sized hole in clarity. She pulled me close into her arms.

"I told myself that as soon as I could afford a place to live and an education for you, I would go back for you," Eindra whispered in my ear.

"What happened?" I lifted up my head to ask.

"Even if I did save enough money, I could never get a hukou for you to go to school."

"Why did you leave us?"

"I had no choice but to come find work. You father gambled away all his wages from the factory."

We sat in silence for a little while.

"When you make a lot of money will you buy your way back to me?" I asked her.

"If I make a lot of money, I will buy you the world," my mother promised.

I remembered almost throwing up, being handed two white pills, and ... that was the last thing I remembered.

"Where?" I asked the driver in my broken Chinese.

"We'll be there in an hour. It's not far," the driver said.

He never told me where we were going; I didn't ask again.

As we neared the bottom of the mountain, I saw withering corn fields rustle in the breeze. People in straw hats were bent over, working in them. We passed a few mud brick houses, a market full of people selling things, children playing on the streets, old folks playing mahjong near a tea shop before we stopped at a brick house. I got out of the car, pausing to observe. This one was bigger than the ones beside it. They had a dirty white dog standing in front of maroon doors. Compared to the mud brick houses, this one seemed fancier.

Maybe that meant they'd pay me more; maybe it meant I'd have more work to do; maybe both.

"Come now, they're waiting for you," said the driver, ushering me forward. I hesitantly walked, my legs cramping from sitting still for so long.

A woman three times my width opened up the doors wearing a frown.

"Hi, my name is Dolkar. I'm here to work for you." I tried to appear friendly, putting together some words I thought made sense. Sometimes I could pick apart words I understood in certain sentences, but still not understand the full conjugation.

"Little girl knows her place," she approved, the faintest of smiles on her mouth, never reaching her eyes. "Come." She gestured.

I followed.

Inside, it was bright. Floors were white. Couches had pink and green sheets layering over them. Neat, fairly clean. A round man with huge moles on his face sat at the end of the couch playing a game on his phone; he hardly noticed us walking in.

"And this is your husband," the woman introduced, pointing at the round man.

My what?

she said nothing

Idalia

A general, fundamental difference between Western and Eastern culture: things being stated versus things being implied; outspoken versus mild people. There was no right, no wrong way of doing things. Simply different.

When Tashi's father fell ill with a stroke, the right thing to do was to go back and help out as soon as school ended for the holidays. Tashi never asked me to; he didn't need to. It was just the right thing to do.

In the two weeks I was there, I made myself as useful as I could. I took calls, I scheduled guests, I dealt with complaints from unsatisfied customers. It wasn't necessarily more work than what I was used to, it wasn't that they piled anything up on me—it was the emotional drainage that bled me dry. What I once saw were the most vibrant of lives became a desolate attempt to keep things normal. And when everyone was spread out thin, trying extra hard to "keep things normal," it was doubly exhausting. Things weren't normal. The investment garnered up in Vietnam for a replica of this resort had been blasted into ashes; money poured out like water.

Employees, most of them from rural villages in the countryside, feared for their jobs. What I saw were the happiest people alive all of a sudden turned overly sensitive at times; one bad joke could instigate fury, one snide comment could end badly.

It was a place that had lost its luster. It was a place I worked hard to survive through the day.

I was lying to Tashi's mother, Mrs. Norzin, when I told her how much I wanted to be there. At home, though my parents always had the intention to make me do chores, every time I had a test or a track meet or art class or even a quiz, I got out of chores faster than you could say "fast."

Sitting there doing chores for my boyfriend's family, all I felt was shame. I was ashamed that all those years my parents took care of every single little thing. My dad always fixed anything that needed fixing—a bike, a light, the A/C, my life—the lawn was forever mowed, and so far none of us went to prison for evading taxes. The cars were always maintained.

The first time something was wrong with my car in college, I had to call my dad at work. What was he supposed to do? I eventually fixed it, only to wreck it six months later. My mom cooked the most balanced, delicious, nutritious meals ever, and the little brat that I was had the audacity to point out if something had too much salt or was too bland or whatever my ungrateful self thought. The fridge or the bathroom never lacked anything I needed, and everything miraculously found a place for itself. Seeing that these seemingly minimal tasks didn't magically do themselves, I wanted to run to my parents and give them a hug.

I wanted to go home. I wanted to go back to my parent's house and not have to pretend I was as understanding, as tolerant, as *nice and sacrificial* as I was acting.

I wanted to go home. I wanted to go back to my parent's house and not have to pretend to follow every step of the recipe like I was a good cook. I was actually terrible, but my mom always had a plan B or corrected my disasters in the kitchen.

I wanted to go home. I was tired of being *this* careful—afraid of doing something wrong, afraid of saying something insensitive, afraid of them thinking I was not doing enough. I tiptoed through my every interaction.

Two days before I was scheduled to leave, I was ready to cry. On my way to the stone well to get "natural spring water" like the new customer had demanded, I was irate at the nerve of him. I had patiently explained that we drink bottled water here like every other homestay or hotel.

"Didn't you advertise 'all things organic' in your flyer?" the customer remarked impatiently.

"Yes sir, we do have a well, and our own gardens. Everything out there *is* organic, but that's for you to enjoy when you're out in the field. Usually our customers head to the well after they've had a rough afternoon hiking, horseback riding, or picking vegetables from the garden. We don't have room service here."

"I want it in my room, *immediately*," he quietly demanded, undoing his tie and crossing his arms.

"I'm sorry, I can make an exception for you and bring you a pack of bottled water. Carrying spring water all the way here is simply not a service we provide," I explained in as even a tone as I could manage.

SHE SAID NOTHING · 229

"With the time you spent standing here uselessly you could've been back with the water by now. You don't understand what I can do to your business, do you?"

I didn't have it in me to argue or stand up for myself; I didn't want to create trouble for Tashi or Jun's family. "Okay, I'll bring it to you in twenty minutes."

It was a ten-minute walk from the stables to his room. He wanted two entire buckets. Love was supposed to be sacrifice, I knew, but I could not stand this anymore. *Jeff Bezos probably doesn't have an attitude; Bill Gates is out there saving the world; Warren Buffet is as humble as can be, who did this guest think he was? Christian Grey?*

The heaviness I felt didn't come from just him, it was rather the solemn environment that cascaded after Mr. Norzin's stroke, enveloping Mrs. Norzin in misery, which spread like a wildfire.

Panting with the two buckets in my arms, I stopped for a second to breathe. I could not get myself to move, and it had nothing to do with being out of shape, though that might've been true too. I gasped. A split second was all it took for my life to flash before my eyes. And it was scary. *These two weeks, they would be my life if ... if I stay with him.* Helping out his family was an unspoken duty in these tumultuous times. If everything had been the way it was before the incident, I could fly off and start my career wherever I wanted it to be, for the world was at my feet and my priority was myself. We could figure something out together. But with *this*, what kind of person would I be if I didn't stay?

This resort was one of a kind, and I used to love it there, but without its former glory, without Mr. Norzin's business and government connections, it was faltering by the second.

The doors that opened for them now were through pity, I could tell, not through value proposition.
What happens when pity runs out?
I cannot stay here; my heart will die, and all Tashi would have would be a shell of a body. Twenty-two. I'm too young to have never attempted fighting to see the world and losing it at the same time.
I can't. I can't. He's great, but …
But what Idalia?
But I can't stay here all my life. I mean look at Mr. Norzin—I'm sorry to think, but he'll likely only get worse. What about *my* family? Wouldn't they want me around?
Is it your family or yourself? Because they didn't raise you up to be a selfish little hoe.
Is there anything wrong with prioritizing myself? If I don't prioritize myself and my happiness, I'll only be a negative influence to anyone around me.
I mean, no, there's nothing wrong. It's not about right and wrong.
You sure as hell are making it seem like this is a choice between right and wrong. Look. Let's set our eyes to a decade down the line. I'd be unhappy, I'd be unsatisfied. Discontent. This relationship would spiral down the toilet. On top of dealing with his dad's health bills and taking care of the resort, he'd have to deal with me. In the long run, if I didn't prioritize myself, I'd only end up hindering him.
Oh …
Yeah. So shut up, Ms. Holier Than Thou.
After I delivered the water, I walked through the rest of my day like I was on steroids. All my neurons were entangled; all my neurotransmitters stopped signaling. The next thing I knew, I was sitting across from Tashi on the eve of

our last day together. He had picked out a hotpot restaurant, my favorite.

"Happy birthday." I raised my Pinot Noir to a toast. In my deep V-neck, wine-red dress, I glanced at how dashing he was in navy blue; I spent two precious seconds agonizing over how perfect we looked together. *Looked.* Not how perfect we were.

"How did you know?" His eyes sparkled, the only solid in the wave of heat coming up from the pot.

I clung to that clarity—*if I don't do it now, I'd never be able to do it.* I knew what I had to do, but I was shaking. The number of times that I counted down could've sent man to the moon so many times man would've started a moon base. I could only compare this to bungee jumping. When I went bungee jumping, every cell in my body told me: *Idalia, you are stupid. Do not jump. This is suicidal.* Every natural instinct in my body told me to save myself. I did it anyways, and the adrenaline afterwards was insane. But *this?* This was infinitely harder; every cell in my body told me: *Idalia, don't break your own heart. Do not do it.*

But I had to! I began. "Tashi, I ..."

He put down his chopsticks to look at me. I felt like regret was about to come and dig my heart out of my chest.

I paused, unable to meet his eyes. I looked down and shut my eyes tight. I shook my head, looked back up, did everything I possibly could to prolong the time before what I had to do next.

"I'm sorry, I ..."

I vowed I wouldn't cry in front of him; I vowed I'd keep my head high, and yet the tears spilled, disobeying my dignity.

"I understand," he began.

The fact that it registered in him what I meant, unspoken, hurt me more than if he had slapped me.

"Don't. *Don't* understand. I'm a coward. I'm a disgrace to mankind. I don't deserve another good thing in life. My mother would be ashamed of me—she sacrificed everything for love. You should be yelling at me! You should hate me! You should despise me, tell me I'm a materialistic bitch. I'm giving up on us—for something I can't even pinpoint."

He took a second to let me calm down. Even that tiny gesture fractured my already broken heart into more pieces. He was so kind.

"You're young, Idalia. It's my fault. I promised you the world, but I'll be the one to chain you down from it. If you hadn't brought this up, *I* would've asked you to never come back. You made it easier for me."

I stared at him both in silence and in awe. They say a breakup really magnifies someone's character. If this was true, I was letting go of gold.

He walked toward my seat, bending down close to me; he lifted my chin upward, that I might look at him, and gently wiped away my tears. "Go, get out of here. Leave and never come back. Within your eyes I see the entire galaxy, but it's also a world I can barely fit into. I've never met someone who lit their life up with that much passion. You can't be constrained, baby, there's no way. I'd be damned if I were the one to kill the life in you. Go live the way you were meant to live."

I said nothing. My heart said everything.

* * *

pg. 19

nothing
i said nothing
all i could manage to say was
nothing?

woman, cold-hearted is my name

well
cold-hearted i shall be
then
farewell,
good riddance

that very night i
bought a one-way ticket to Venezuela
left his magnolias out to die
and never turned back

she had the world within her eyes, and you—
you had her

you gave her all your love and
all she gave you in return
was that bottle of Pinot Noir and the
magnolias she left out to die

woman, cold-hearted is thy name

Avici

Dolkar

In the day, I cleaned and cooked. I did everything. When I'd refuse to keep going after twelve hours of working, this woman slapped me. Her name was Suo Xiu. She was to be my mother-in-law.

The first time I talked back, asking how much I'd get paid, she banged my head into the wall.

The entire village revered her because her nephew was the chief of police, and his dad was the chief before him.

The second time I asked if I could call my mom, she tugged my hair, handfuls of it coming out in locks.

The entire village revered her because her husband sent back enough money from the city to buy them everything they needed, so she didn't need to work in the field like the rest of them did.

The third time I said something she didn't want to hear, she threw a broomstick at me.

This was the essence of my days. And it was nothing compared to my nights.

The son of the Suo (maternal last name) and Zhu (paternal last name) clans, the one introduced to me as my *husband*—he would come back from the police station where he worked; I'd long since developed a mood detector. Did something happen to dampen his mood? What was it? Was it his boss? Did he get a bonus this month? Did he drink yet? Would tonight be the night where I'm left alone? Where I could sleep on the floor?

Usually, the first time he came back was okay. He'd drop in and then go back out for beers with his friends.

It was the second time I was terrified of. I didn't know what hour of the night it could be. He could come back any second. I'd lay awake, dreading it. Each second that ticked by, I shuddered a little more violently. I also wished he'd be back sooner because the earlier it was, the less aggressive he seemed to be. There I was, praying for him to be back sooner so it could be over quicker. There I was, trembling for fear *it* would be soon.

Once, I begged him to stay so he wouldn't have the chance to get drunk. He looked at me like I was a dirty piece of gum stuck on his shoe, sneered, and walked out. I never asked again.

Along with a mood detector, I also developed an internal clock aligning his behavior with the time. If it was before midnight, he usually left me alone. After 4 a.m., he always hit the pillow snoring as soon as he came in. Two in the morning was a done deal: the peak of my torture.

From wherever I was, no matter where I was hiding, he'd find me. He'd drag me into our room, grab my arm roughly, and throw me on the bed.

"Open up," he'd growl. I squeezed my eyes shut and laid limp until he was done.

"I said loosen up," he'd grunt. I wondered if his reincarnation was butchered—as in he was supposed to be on the path to become a human, but it didn't work out completely, leaving him to be half a beast.

I continued laying there stiffly, inured to this monstrosity; he'd shake me harder, grasping my legs and pulling me apart, pissed that I ruined his climax.

If he didn't get it, he'd grab the belt on the floor and start beating, always silently. I wondered if Naraka would be better than this. If I was so bad I was sent to Naraka, at least it would make sense for me to be there. Here? It made no sense why I was suffering so. In those moments, I found myself wondering if Tashi had done this on purpose. And if he did, I wondered why, what did I do to deserve it?

No amount of pleading ever worked. No amount of screaming ever worked; I could've been dying, and no one would come in to stop him. It wasn't that I hadn't tried. One night, I locked myself in the bathroom with a kitchen knife and a bowl of warm water. I looked at my face in the mirror, eight shades lighter. My hands were balled into fists, and I shivered. *It's now or never.* I thought about my mom. I did not want to die. I would give anything to be in my mom's arms again, knowing that she'd been working extra shifts for years to get back to me, that she was probably working her way through a night shift right then to buy her way to me.

I was not suicidal. I did not *desire* death—it was freedom I was seeking.

One slice on my wrist and into the warm water my hand went. I smiled softly. *Sleep now*, I heard my mom say in my dreams.

* * *

I woke up in bed, thinking if this was death then let me stay here forever.

That was before Xiu's face towered above mine. "You're awake?"

I opened my eyes. She died too?

"Don't you dare try something like that again," she threatened.

I did try again. Many times more. Each time I sliced deeper than before, but then they started taking all the knives to Xiu's bedroom.

* * *

I tried running before I tried cutting, though I quickly found out why they had no need to keep me chained.

When Xiu sent me to the market to buy pork, or celery, or whatever it was she needed, I took the chance to escape to the next village.

Just as I neared the junction between where village houses ended and fields started appearing, a man shouted loudly. "Hey you! Aren't you the bride the Suo family bought?"

Several people glanced up from their chairs, and all three of them ran after me.

Next, I made the mistake of asking the village chief for help.

He sighed, looked at me in pity, and all he said was, "There's nothing I can do."

"But why? You hear me screaming at night, I know you do. Why? It doesn't take a genius to piece together what they're doing to me."

He went silent, looking down, unable to meet my eyes.

"Help me. Please. I'm begging you. I will get down on my knees if you want me to."

"No, no, no don't do that." He stopped me halfway; he finally confessed softly under his breath, "I'll tell you why. The entire Suo family will threaten my own—they all pooled in money to buy you."

"Why did they do this?"

"To ensure social order."

* * *

When I found out I was pregnant, things got better for a brief period. Xiu smiled brightly at my belly, telling me my job was to gain fat and let this little one grow.

When I bent down to mop the floors, she quickly ran over and told me she'd do it. "Go rest, go rest," she'd instruct.

I shifted from one foot to the other. I did not believe her. I went to the kitchen to prepare lunch.

"No, no, I can do that."

It felt surreal.

I could lay in bed all day or watch TV. Meat was prepared for me in every meal. I don't think I'd eaten that much in my whole life.

"Eat, here. This fish is good for the baby's brain," Xiu pestered me with every day, overfilling my bowl.

They went so far as to let me take my best friend, the stray dog I'd been secretly caring for, inside after I washed him. His name was Tofu, a sweet, white, intelligent little Japanese Spitz, abandoned; I first met him when I arrived, his white fur tainted a dirty brown. I couldn't say I liked the human race too much—Tofu and I, we got along. He was the best

AVICI · 239

and only friend I ever had; he gave all his loyalty to me and trusted me completely. We spent most of our time sitting next to each other silently. With eyes purer than my own, he watched out for me, but even his barks couldn't prevent the inevitable from happening.

I was five weeks pregnant when he barged in at 2 a.m., drunk out of his mind.

I thought I would be safe until I delivered this baby, but this time was no different than all the others, except this time my body couldn't take it.

"Open up." He shoved me mercilessly.

"Please, I have your child," I stammered.

He went in. I started screaming.

For once, Xiu came to stop him. "Are you crazy!" She shoved him away from me.

He pushed her aside.

"You are out of your goddamn mind!" Xiu screamed, pushing him back again.

Back and forth they shoved; every time I sat up, he pinned me roughly to the bed. He then pushed his mother so hard her body slammed against the wall with a deafening *bang*.

"You pig. You'll end your bloodline, once and for all, just like all the other times!" she retaliated.

He drove her out the door and locked it behind her. She banged on it so intensely I felt the house shake. Next, he eyed me.

And continued.

When I resisted, he picked up his belt.

I bled all the way to the hospital. I felt knives stab through my body, and bit back the agony. My throat was already hoarse. Everything hurt, so much so that I would stop sensing, and then when my body sent reports back to my brain again, knives turned into power saws slicing me in half across my stomach. The sharp ache through my sciatic nerve never quit piercing me through the night.

By the time the terrible intensity subsided, my period of bliss was over. Xiu looked at me with disgust, like I was a stray dog she'd kick out of her way in the streets. Useless to her. Vegetables were back on the dinner table; I could barely pick out egg and tomato crumbs in the soup they left for me. I went back to cleaning the bathroom or washing all the sheets using a wooden washboard in the back of the house.

* * *

Tofu was thrown onto the streets once more. I'd go visit him as often as I could, but lately I had been seeing him less and less. When I went to the market that day, I searched through all the streets he would usually be on, high and low, and could not find him.

I started getting worried.

"Tofu!" I called out.

A week later, he met me at our front door, his head down, whimpering. When he looked up at me, his tail sagging, rasping for the next laborious breath, I felt a part of myself dying. *No*, not Tofu. Anyone but Tofu. I looked him all over. No bleeding. Nothing abnormal. Only everything was wrong.

I held him tightly in my arms. "Stay with me, stay with me!" I cried.

I carried him inside to beg Xiu to let me take him to the hospital.

"They treat humans at the hospital, not stray dogs."

"I know, but there isn't a vet anywhere around. Let me ask a doctor—one of them might know how to treat a dog,"

I sobbed. At this point I couldn't speak clearly. "Please!" I threw my knees on the ground. Crawling one knee in front of the other to her feet, I tugged at the hem of her red shirt as she sat at the couch, not even glancing my way.

Xiu's son, eyes still glued to the TV, chimed in nonchalantly. "Just let her. Not like they could do anything about a dog."

I sprinted down the street to the hospital, as gently as I could without shuffling Tofu. "Tofu, not yet. I know you're tired. Stay with me."

I asked everyone in white if they could please take a look at him and see what was wrong. They would not even glance our way. Finally, a patient rolling by in a wheelchair told me he would try to find what's wrong; he said he'd trained a few dogs before. I set Tofu down in his lap. He lightly brushed his fingers across Tofu's fur, listening to him breathe. He shook his head.

If there really was a state of Nirvana somewhere where there was no pain and no suffering, Tofu deserved it more than anyone.

When I buried him where the red fern grew, I buried myself with him.

inchoate vignettes

Idalia

pg. 20

i think i have words now

he once told me to
go
get out
go make a name for myself and
never
look
back
how could i?

i said nothing
only heartlessly flew far, far away
perhaps some time later
i might finally be able to "live

the way (i was) meant to live"
whatever that means

the "thank you" that i didn't but should've said
a million times over
i am paying back with my life
plus interest
it's weird now that i think about it—i can easily
say thank you and sorry to a million strangers
a hundred times each
why was it impossible with you?

i had too much pride
i took your admiration for granted
thinking that's how it's supposed to be
justifying myself with "confidence"

i had been too reckless
i took your tolerance for granted
thinking that's how it's meant to be
justifying myself with "fearless"

it's my heart that was too wild
i took your patience for granted
thinking i was merely being "ambitious"
justifying myself with "realistic"

forgive me for being this way
i don't know what other way
i could be

pg. 21: me me and me

only me

they say vienna is the city of dreams
and venice is the bride of the sea
lima, city of kings and
tivoli, city of delights—
xi'an, my love, ancient capital of civilization
los angeles, city of angels, I fancy you—alas,
where shall I go?
what should I do?
how shall I live?

I think the best part about traveling alone
is the redefinition
meeting up with parts of myself I thought
    were beyond lost
where before, his opinion mattered because I cared,
the only opinion that matters now is my own
who am I? where am I? who will I possibly be?
I don't know
neither am I required to know
that's one kind of freedom I'll never tire of

one guy I met trades crypto as he treks through
Europe, muy chévere bro!
told this girl I travel as an author!
why? it was the first thing I blurted out
am I? not really
does it matter? not at all
for that one moment: business? business

who? corporate America, do I know you?
investments-i-don't-need-to-
know-about and pretensions-i-don't-need-to-cater to, when
in "real life" heck yeah I should be grinding

in my career, I've always felt behind some kind of standard
hard skills-wise: where it took some people a few hours to understand something as simple as a straightforward
accounting concept, it took me days
soft-skills-wise: where expressing themselves and connecting with others seemed like it flowed naturally to
people, it took massive truckloads of effort to get me to even speak
why shouldn't i feel behind?

why am i here?

in Russia, if I wanted to be an author, then author I would be
in Spain, if I wanted to take a Spanish class, then Spanish class I would be taking
in Chile, if I wanted to dance, then dancing I would be doing
I could be a travel blogger for all they know—in Ethiopia
they would know—at home
they wouldn't approve—at home
"im not good enough" i say

did i ask you? if i want to, i simply will
at home? not so much
i "should be" getting those financial concepts
down
i "should be" getting a certificate on Power BI
or whatever the buzz is these days
i "should be" applying for programs and jobs
i "should be" this and that, that and this, i
"should" have my life together
shouldn't it be MY life?

and yes all these experiences were breathtaking,
I wouldn't trade them for the world but no I did
not have the
most glamorous time of my life
there were definitely moments when the
silence became too deafening
pain too much to bear
loneliness too bewildering to carry
yet the moments of pure happiness, insanity
the kindness I met along the way, electrifying:
the group of backpackers who led me back to the
trail in Abisko,
woman who saved me from an hour of walking in
a snowstorm,
guy who stopped in the middle of the highway to give
me a ride as I was lugging a suitcase across town,
receptionist who brought my debit card up to my room,
man who lent me skis for free because I was about to
cry when the northern lights weren't showing up,
guy who built us a fire as we sat around talking
Cambodia's politics

i'm a lucky one; I've only ever been met with
kindness, overwhelming kindness, everywhere
I've gone
that
in itself
is Grace

pg. 22: the healing saga

hey
it's been awhile
i will go ahead and admit it:
yes, i purposely skip your Instagram stories
    because I...
i guess i want to trick myself into believing i
    don't care...
at all
not even a little bit

hey
it's been awhile
i ran into you the other day
fine i guess it wasn't "ran into"... what else
would I be doing in your city? traveling? please.
i said i'd never tell you i'm here
i said i'm only here for the fresh air
i said a lot of things to let myself go
i didn't run into you until the very last day—
when everyone who knew us already told you i
was here

we smiled at each other, a lifetime of emotions
mirroring our features
you opened up the conversation: "I heard you
finally met the human rights lawyer you admire."
I tend to say nothing a lot nowadays
I did do that—that and a lot of other cool things
but who will sit here and account for the costs for
me?
I did not need an accountant to know that he
was a sunk cost—anything I do from here on out
is either an
investment or a return—he should never be part
of the equation
you continued: "I know I'm months too late,
but congratulations on your job—I know it's
everything you wanted."
"thank you," I finally said something
I did not tell him I quit that job and am looking
for one I will love more than I loved him
I did not tell him that
in my mind I knew
it was less about chasing the money
more about filling up an empty house with crazy
schedules
because as long
as
it ended the slow and endless drizzle
because as long
as
it ended the passive aggressive voices
because as long
as

i could fall asleep at night
i'd be okay
for another day

I broke the long silence: "they all gossip about
me—they say I drove you away by pride, that
I'm the reason why
I'm still not married."
"They're not ... wrong," he laughed
I frowned, then smiled as I looked out to see a
couple riding on "our" horse, basked in the light
of dusk, happy
he's back to being himself
"hey, look at me," he was serious again, searching
for my gaze like all the times he's done before,
except this
time he couldn't touch me, "your show's
merely getting started. let them talk. they don't
understand you and you
don't need them to."
only *you* would protect me like that, as if it's second
nature—you should be the one who hates me most
I think he understood my dilemma—he
continued
"but if you had really succumbed, you wouldn't
have been the girl I loved"
"loved ... oh"
oh no, did I say that out loud?
"the woman I admire, still"

and my heart is echoing that piercing phrase,
long after your footsteps desert

* * *

pg. 27: Renaissance

I didn't think I still had the capacity for this, but after he awakened the long-dormant romantic in me, I keep replaying how things snowballed at Te & Kaffehuset—how he caught up to me, and—

him: hey, you single?
me: yeah ...
him: good. seeing anyone?
me: no
him, walking closer to me: perfect. look at me. are you interested?
me: no
him: well you're about to be
I pointed up my chin to say—try me. He looked into my eyes in a "I take that as a challenge" type of way. Then I couldn't help it, I laughed, perfectly caught in his charm.
He's seems ... dangerous. Like he's been through London Exchange, wrecked them all, and walked out to build a life he actually wants to live
He looks like I have a lot to learn from him.

pg. 27: on last night

alas i learned
how faithful my heart is

how faithful it is even when it no longer needs to be
faithful
whether this is virtue or vice i do not know
i'm afraid this might
end up being
vice

i know being emotionally careless can be a very
empowering status
just think of the "french woman"
she's free, she's fast, she's elegant, she's effortless,
no strings attached
she spreads romance for the night and goes back to
being her independent opinionated self for the day
she has splendid taste: wine, cheese, art, music,
history, she knows it all
the people she knows and the things she's seen, insane
i thought she was an ideal until i went to Paris
and met Parisian women who really encompass
the ideal

... but
last night
oh dear God last night
when the Te & Kaffehuset guy leaned in to kiss me ...
my mind can lie all it wants but my body cannot
i turned away
it would've been such fun, i know
the Swedish Lapland: land of the Aurora
Borealis, of reindeer so many and snow so thick
the ambiance was perfect: cheese and cognac,
marshmallows and rum, and the fire he made to

keep me warm
he'd been dropping hints all night, hints i
ignored at first because i thought he always does this
i thought it was just him, y'know, a habit, almost
very Wall Street-esque
i asked him if this is what he does all the time
he goes, do what?
i say, take girls to your room and taste cheese
and wine with them
he said, no i can sincerely count on my one
hand the number of times this happened
i doubt it
he saw that and said: you're about to choose to
not believe me
thanks, Sherlock
what makes you think I'll believe you?

but
oh God, his hints
asking me if i'm single; yeah, i said; well
enchanté, said he
hand on my waist as we stood watching the moon
touches lingering longer than necessary
asking me, "why do you keep moving away when
i get closer"; i said it was a natural instinct
and "what are you thinking?"; i bonked the
question back to him

and afterwards
when i dodged, i tried to explain why i didn't
want it
i said, no it's not you. it's me. it's just been

INCHOATE VIGNETTES · 253

years since i ... i was taken by surprise
he was respectful about it all, such a gentleman
and the cigarette smoke blown toward me, an act
of flirtation, he explained when i coughed
and "look at me, in my eyes"; i hid my face in
my hands
he said, "what are you afraid of?"; i said nothing
"tell me"
i shook my head and just said "you're so close i
can't think"
"then don't"
the magical thing about it all is, we connect, we
really did
he knows me, understands me, and i him
how could i not?
he saw a picture of the northern lights, decided
he wanted to see it, and went
decided he liked it there
and stayed
he manifested my dream
his stories of the world: Belize, Nicaragua,
Chile, Indonesia, Laos ...
his tattoo of his—what seemed to me like a world tour
he has lived my dream

but i thought our chemistry was friendship
he understands the way i think and i him
there's an effortless flow
and clearly he was not looking for a relationship
neither was i
it would've been so fun
but my body dodged it before my mind could lie

to me
no i didn't want it
my heart was elsewhere
the boy who i was supposed to be over long ago
it was his face i saw the second he leaned in
it was his face i wanted to see
his voice in my mind, his body i wanted to feel
my instinct was to turn away, my heart knew it wasn't him
and thus i realized
no
i'm still not over him
how capricious can i possibly be
the lucid truth flashes screaming colors in my face: he! will! never! again! be! yours!
my mind has moved on a million times but
when push comes to shove
i still chose my heart
because had it been him who leaned in last night
and me, fully acknowledging we will never again <u>be</u>
i
would have
let him
kiss me
till daybreak
because had it been him who leaned in last night
and me, fully acknowledging how much my visions mean to me, how much i'm willing to sacrifice for my
ambitions
all he had to do was call my name and
i

INCHOATE VIGNETTES · 255

would have
followed him
to the ends of the earth
every time i blatantly lied to myself, telling myself
maybe i should move to his city because scenery is
beautiful
there
every
single
time
my heart leaped forward but my mind stopped
my hands from booking the ticket
i like him too much
things will happen
so i had to, had to get out of our cities
go toward a new world
see how small i am compared to God's majesty
and realize
who the heck is he when i don't even know who i am
i'll fall deeper and
deeper and
deeper in
Love with
myself

pg. 28 ineffable

your heart, a vignette:
you don't need to know where i am because
all i want to be
is where i cannot be

i see him everywhere
everywhere i'm not supposed to
he has infused himself into my worldview
without ever meaning to
without me proactively thinking about it
in the eyes of the most adorable child sitting next
to me in a café—Tatte, in DC—could've been ours
I didn't want children
I didn't think I could be a good mother—I
wanted to be one more than anything—yet
I'm terrified they'd turn out like me
and i'd be worried all the time
like my mom
but
I did want to bear our children

i saw him
in the food I chose to order at Reffen
i compared him
to the man I dismissed because he was climbing
the corporate ladder like there was no tomorrow—
you were
never like that
I do love to see purpose
I do admire ambition but
not in the rigid way it's known to be—you
showed me a greater world, a different nuance
for ambition i admire
more than you will ever know

i see him everywhere
everywhere i'm not supposed to

he has infused himself into my worldview and
i think that's beautiful since
he has expanded it
boy, you expanded my mind!

pg. 29: you are a lucky one

oh to be loved by her
love is innocently pure
divinely beautiful
tenaciously adamant
unlike anything you've ever experienced
you're alive in her thoughts even when she's busy with
data to analyze
deliverables to turn in
presentations to prepare for
investments to research
you're alive in her thoughts
in the midst of her plans she's
subconsciously whispering your name
in the words she puts together on paper
in the scenes she reenacts before her eye lids close
in the worlds she creates
you live on and
all you had to do was
breathe

oh to be loved by her
you're not her world nor will you ever be but
until she moves on

you're brighter than the brightest star in the galaxy
you thank God
for whatever it was that led you to her heart
because in her thoughts you
really start to live in ways
you never thought were possible
ways that defy quantum physics
ways that make time limitless
you become the luckiest person in the world but
now
you
will
never
find out for
she keeps all her pain to
herself and
oh God how could she sleep when
you were her dream when
your voice was all she heard when
you kept her up till 3 a.m.
sipping rosé
staring up at the moon
wishing you
nothing but the very best

* * *

And with that, I sealed him out of my heart forevermore. Next epoch, begin.

Mr. Jim Raleigh

"هَلْ جَزَآءُ ٱلْإِحْسَٰنِ إِلَّا ٱلْإِحْسَٰنُ"

—QURAN 55:60

Arno

After that escapade in the police office, I felt like a joke. Nothing had been planned out correctly.

All I knew was I'd take Dolkar to the police station of Zhengzhou, the capital of this province. I thought they'd likely have more developed systems and responsible officers. What would Carlisle and I have done once we got there? Throw her to the police officers?

The plan was supposed to be: I would steal Dolkar away and take her to the city, and Carlisle would stay behind so as to not arouse suspicion with the rest of the village and finish the teaching, and then we'd meet in Zhengzhou.

Reality was: I was stuck here without a goddamn idea how to make this situation better. I'd made it worse for Dolkar, and she was probably sitting at home cursing me right that minute. Her family likely had her in chains by then.

I was too late to tell Mr. Raleigh thank you. I still remembered his booming laugh as he tried to reenact the guillotine used in the Reign of Terror during the French Revolution. I still remembered his "Jo Mama" jokes—no, it wasn't yo mama, it was jo mama, for whatever reason. That was just him. I still remembered the debates he set up. Once, the topic was about Christopher Columbus. "Should we remember him as a conqueror or a villain?" he posed to us.

I never knew Columbus as someone who mutilated and enslaved indigenous peoples prior to Mr. Raleigh's class; all I knew was that he sailed the ocean blue in 1492. I had been silent all throughout the class, but someone who was on my own team, arguing Columbus was a hero, said something stupid that irked me. They said the cutting off of hands, ears, lips was a thousand percent reprehensible, but it was not unique to Columbus—it was the status quo of colonization. As if that justified it.

I shot up against the guy on my side. "Did you really just say that? Just because that was the status quo does not make it *right*." We clearly lost the debate, but I can still remember the proud expression Mr. Raleigh had on his face as I said that, and it was everything I needed to feel worthy again.

Me trying to help Dolkar out, was it out of regret for how I'd ended things? As if good karma would wipe out my guilt? Was it for my own ego, to prove I became more than the slums I was stuck in? That someone else was in a deeper slum?

I could not believe myself. Did I really think this whole thing would be as simple as taking her to a police station in a bigger city and packing my bags to go back to my life of privilege?

What the fuck is wrong with me. I'm the one who needs saving. She's the resilient one.

In the midst of my thoughts, I heard two light knocks. A student of ours handed Carlisle a note:

I was never legally registered as his wife.

free

"*להם ושיש... חיים להם שיש יתכן ...בא אני אבל*
חיים הרבה עוד"

—ג׳ון 10:10

Idalia

"Bloody putain!" I screamed, jumping up from bed as the 8:20 flashing across my phone mocked my lazy ass. How many times did I hit snooze?

I just landed my dream job leading the global strategy and acquisition efforts at CX Group, a publishing house headquartered in New York. All the physical books they published were made of recycled material, and although they were a for-profit corporation, they made significant investments into education around the world.

Their vision aligned with my own: if one day I lived in a world where children had equal access to education, I would go sail the seven seas in celebration. *Mierde*, I thought, dropping my binders as I struggled to put on my black editor-looking boots. If I sprinted down those streets like Godzilla was after me, I could try to still make it.

The subway gave me some time to breathe. New York subway. Oxymoron? Quite the contrary. That's how breathless I was. Since moving to New York three days ago, I'd received my fair share of cold glares when I tried to show a little Southern hospitality. I'd been shoved in elevators and subways and frankly everywhere else with too many people, and had doors slammed in my face when I was raised with the notion that you always hold the door for the person behind you. Ah, but in this city that never sleeps, I had opportunity to work on my visions till daybreak.

I had no excuses to be running late; I should know better. Last night was a late night of recording, fixing software problems—more like fixing my "no clue how to use this software" problems and proceeding to alternate between YouTube tutorials and "style through the decades" or "Um you really need to see this hot doctor and his dog" videos.

Let them think I'm laissez-faire, it'll be okay. I'll strut in like Miranda from Devil Wears Prada, *take off those shades, and smile like the sunshine was lugged to them all the way up from Texas. They'll love me.*

The next minute, I was nearing the street corner of my office. I glanced at my watch, 8:50 a.m. Somehow the stars all aligned. The subway must've synced with the bus; chances were next to nothing, as close to nothing as a global pandemic that would send the whole world into quarantine.

Crazy how lucky I was; today was my day. I had a few minutes to grab a coffee, but I couldn't decide between a Matcha Creme Frappuccino or an Iced Americano as I stepped up to order.

"Welcome to Starbucks, what can I get you?"

I was still staring—staring with that glazed-over look you get when you're thinking and some random person reckons you're staring *at* them. Americano put me in deep focus mode but I couldn't drink it too much or I'd start relying on it, while all the Frappuccino does is taste good ... but happiness incentivizes focus, so ...

"A ... a Matcha Americano please," I stuttered as my words registered in my mind while my mouth took a drive on its own.

I buried my head in my other hand for a second as the barista sympathized. "Early morning?"

It wasn't even all that early and not to mention, I was running late thirty minutes ago. He couldn't exactly say "long day" could he? Instead, I chuckled and settled on, "Only getting started. I meant the Iced Americano." Nope, I didn't deserve happiness this morning.

Coffee in one hand, binders in the other, I dug through my purse as my phone rang. A friend of mine, based in Scandinavia. She worked in the marketing department of the automobile industry in Germany (automobile industry? Germany? Crazy! Unheard of.) before leaving corporate altogether to pursue travel. She was thirty-one but looked and felt twenty-three. Her style was timeless; she studied fashion at uni. She lived the way I wanted to one day live. She'd been all over the world, all while working as an independent graphic designer. Her client stream flowed as steadily as she cared to make it. In other words, she was good, real good, at her job. She was even better at living.

We met in Guatemala, right before I jumped off a cliff into Lake Atitlán. No, not suicidal purposes. Cliff diving. Locals did it all the time. Anyhow, our friendship was effortless. We understood each other upon first glance, without a single word.

I felt like a carrot being pulled out of the dirt the first time I talked to Demi; she did the pulling.

After exchanging pleasantries, she asked me what career I was heading into.

"Finance."

"You like that?" Demi had questioned. She later told me she questioned it because creativity was written all over my face.

"I ... don't dislike it. I think I need to spend a few years honing in on the basics of business, make money first, and then I can think about what I like or dislike."

"Bullshit."

Um, I ... what?

Dem was the one who convinced me I needed to deconstruct my value system: it wasn't about making money, killing myself to squeeze in those long hours so I'd have the leverage to quit my job, for the very concept was the definition of entrapment. I could not measure how far we've really come as a society, but last time I checked, I was not trapped.

Then again, if money is what stimulates motivation for you, if that's what excites you, if you like the game and money is merely a way you keep score, chase it. But it wasn't for me. I was no happier than before as I watched my bank account grow, I felt guilt as I saw it fall more quickly than it needed to, but if it didn't move, I didn't work any harder. I never took money for granted, but if the only reason I wanted to chase it was to buy my freedom to build a life I wanted to live, then there was no need. Go build that life *now*. Using passion.

I'd met too many people in the past few months who were monetizing their passion to disregard that I could be one of them. And thus I realized, everything I learned from traveling could be condensed down to three small words: *I am free.*

Not because I deserved it, not because I did anything to earn it, but since it was already given to me at no cost, there was no reason to live as if I had to go around and earn it *again*. I always had been; it was the voices in my head, the comparisons in my mind, the insecurities, the fear of the unknown, of taking a road less traveled, of trying something different, of being doubted, of not living a trajectory previously carved out for me, and a million other voices that kept me from believing a simple Truth: *I am free.*

Passion presides. And after much experimenting, I have found a way to monetize mine.

The duty was to fight toward a world where *more* people had choices. I would not stop fighting systems until no one is in bondage.

"Hey Dem, what's up," I answered, placing my phone between my ear and shoulder as I opened the Starbucks door, leading back to the busy sidewalks of New York.

"I was just about to wish you good luck! First day of your dream …"

"*Verdammt!*" I cursed as I bumped directly into someone, spilling coffee all over my freshly ironed white blouse. Last time I ironed something, tyrannosaurs were still walking around laying eggs.

I picked up my already-cracked-but-now-probably-even-more-cracked phone. "Sorry, bit of a mess this morning. I'll call you back."

She laughed. "I hear that. Glad I taught you something!"

I glanced at the woman I bumped into. "I am so sorry. Did I get coffee on you too?"

This woman, gorgeous by all standards, had bone structure that could cut, wild brown eyes, thick luscious hair, and beautiful lips that looked like she was trying to learn how to smile again.

"You didn't. It's okay," she assured me.

"I apologize. I'm a wreck today."

She said nothing; she simply bent down to help pick up the binders sprawled around us. As she was reaching this way and that, I couldn't help but notice all those scars on her arm. Dozens. The cuts seemed fresh. I'm not a doctor, but the cuts didn't look years old. Months, perhaps.

I froze. I couldn't equate these scars with the calm, sincere essence of this woman. Should I say something? Would I be intruding? Would I be bringing up a past this woman didn't want to think about? I took a deep breath.

No, no, no. What could I possibly do? She seems fine now. I'm stupid. I'm just hallucinating. I'm more dramatic than most people. She's definitely fine.

No way she's okay. I saw them with my own two eyes. Not a scratch or two. Dozens! I need to say something. I should. No, I will say something. But I won't press it.

I took another deep breath.

"You good?" the woman asked, peering into my glazed over eyes.

"What? Oh! Yes, thank you!" I took over the binders and hesitantly turned around to leave.

Why didn't you say anything?

Each step was getting heavier as I walked toward the door of CX.

You're late on your first day. How the frick. Get in those doors. Do something about the coffee stains. Stay focused.

Next thing I knew, I was running back toward the woman I never got the name of. "Hey, if I'm being rude, please let me know. But I couldn't help but notice the scars on your arms, are *you* okay? Is there anything I can do for you?"

This woman paused, a little taken aback. Then she smiled vibrantly, peered away into the sun, then looked straight into my eyes. "I am, now," she asserted with such confidence and grace that I could only know it to be true. She paused before continuing.

"If only someone had asked me that when I wasn't fine ..." She chuckled, surprising herself; she said that lightly, in the same breath as a stranger would say to someone on the subway, "Wow, I love that book you're reading" or "Hey, your bag is open."

She pointed at my white shirt, now splotched in brown. "Wanna switch?"

My mouth dropped open. "Really?"

"Why not?" she shrugged. "I got done meeting my editor; I'm only going to see my mother from here. You can't possibly go to work in that."

I did not know who she was, what she had been through, what her story was—but what I did know was that she did not merely survive. She conquered.

As we stepped back inside the Starbucks to use their bathroom to change, I told her I would love to buy her a coffee to thank her. It was the least I could do. But, as she noted, I was already running late, so maybe another time. I suddenly had an intense desire to read the story of this woman who, given the tragic past she so obviously endured, only emoted confidence.

"Let's grab dinner tonight?" I suggested.

"I would love that," she agreed, jotting down her number on a napkin grabbed from the counter. "And hey, maybe I'll even tell you about the time I was sold by a man whose smile brought out the gods."

She winked. And with that, she was gone.

epilogue

Dolkar

Dolkar walked lightly, the way she always had. She did not leave an epic mark on this earth like the rest of us, obliviously and carelessly trying to leave a legacy no one *really* cares about. All she had been was a gentle leaf shuffled in the eye of a thunderstorm, a process of the earth we know trespassing into oblivion.

But she understood the truth.

We have a total of two fates: (a) we are born into shackles, or (b) we choose which shackles constrict us. That, we cannot escape.

She chose a third: the ultimate freedom, a panacea for all her suffering. But the Truth she did not understand, was that tomorrow would have been another day—for Joy to find a way.

It always does.

Acknowledgments

I will continue to say it a million times more, thank you:

谢谢你们, 陈晓和魏钰楠。最应该感谢的就是我爸爸妈妈，跨过山，越过海，所以我可以有追梦的自由。是你们的坚持成就了我的坚持; 没有你们也不会有我。

William—thank you for making me laugh, most of the time. We could all use a little joy, and you are always chill when I'm freaking out over nothing. Please don't ever stop being you. Daniel—you are the best gift *ever*. Nothing will surpass how special it was for our birthdays to sync perfectly, twelve years apart.

I love you with all my heart. 是你们的爱支撑着我。爱你们。

奶奶，婶婶，伯伯，哥哥—谢谢你们让我们每次回成都都有家可归。

奶奶，姨妈，大姨夫，姐姐，妈咪，二姨夫，可儿—谢谢你们让西安早就变成了家。

有你们的地方就是家。这边也有我们无时无刻的牵挂。

爷爷——我真的很想你。从小到大我只习惯什么事情都自己解决——唯独你宠过我。

爷爷——听说你的书法出了名的美，可能我对文学的向往离不开你对书法的坚持。

To my friends, thank you. When I choose my friends, it's for life. Gloria—我认定你了, you mean everything to me. You walked through every step with me. You were always patient when I was a frantic mess. Wendy—I didn't know clicking with someone could happen in the first two seconds of meeting, but it did with us. It scares me to think how much I'd be missing if I hadn't met you. Rebecca—remember the days I'd see you every day of every week? We *are* the OG. Carrie—out of everything we've been through together, I don't know why our first car crash is topping my mind. Shirley—you make everything epic; I can't stop laughing whenever I'm with you. Elizabeth—I admire you. I will always fly to whichever city you're in to meet you; you *are* a piece of home. Anna—time with you feels like sunny afternoons sucking on popsicles at the beach, when time slows down and we are simply ourselves. Kristine—I will always admire the strength I see in you. Jenny—you've been nothing but kind, keeping me grounded every week while we prayed together. Zein—only when I saw you again did I realize how beautiful of a person you are, how far you've come since road trips with our families. Doyeon—thank you for listening to my stupid rants the number of times you have. Courtney—your joy is infectious, and I will always love that about you. Tara—wait for me in France. Alli—you are someone it took me two seconds to decide I wanted to be friends with because I saw your heart and how you treat people.

Love and thank you all.

To my teachers, thank you for making me believe in education when I started to lose hope in my place in it. I always loved learning, but it was you who gave me hope when I couldn't see myself as more than a number. Mr. Beckham—I never expected to be calling you years after leaving middle school, but I am so glad I did. Mr. Harris—your class was always the highlight of my day the entire freshman year. I wish I expressed to you more strongly back then how much I truly loved it, but now you'll see when I hand this to you. You opened up my eyes to how fun Shakespeare can be, and part of this book is inspired by what you taught me when we read *To Kill a Mockingbird*. Mr. Filson—you are the only reason I love history; I wish I could hand this to you, but do know that you inspired Arno to do something irrationally kind. You inspire *me* to be some*one* irrationally kind. Mrs. Jasperson—I was on the verge of completely losing my ambition when you agreed to work on TEDx with us. You have only continued to inspire me throughout our time working on it. I admire you and want to be like you.

Dr. A—I will never forget the moment I heard you trying to save my life as I was going down that waterfall. Thank you for taking us around on one of the best trips of my life—you opened my eyes to a world I hadn't known before. David—thank you for looking over my manuscript. I remember taking your Persuasion class spontaneously. That was before you taught me that Peitho, handmaiden to Aphrodite, signifies that to persuade is to be in service of beauty, of something ideal, of an idea we find to be beautiful and want someone else to see as well. Well now I know: the secret to sounding passionate … is to, get this, actually *be* passionate. Revolutionary. Tony and Lisa Okoromadu, thank you both. Tony—thank you for always lending a listening ear and for your advice. Lisa—you agreed to review my manuscript when we've never met, and I will forever be grateful for you. Jenn Rost—you spoke out-loud thoughts I had but wanted to deny; because of you, I will be chasing my dream, I will find a career I love, and I will always look up to you. Thank you.

Thank you to the team at New Degree Press who made this book come alive. Eric Koester—I hope you don't remember my first idea for this book. I don't know why I ever thought that was a good idea. Thank you for developing this brilliant platform. You have made numerous dreams come true, mine being one of them. Ilia Epifanov and Angela Mitchell, thank you for your input, for filling in holes in my plot even when nothing I was saying or writing made sense. Mozelle Jordan, I always feel like you and I are on the same wavelength; I truly treasure that. This book could not stand on its own without you—all the work you've put into editing, your support, believing in it, thank you. Michelle Felich—I thoroughly enjoyed reading all your commentary.

And to everyone who supported me before the book was even out, you made my dream come true. I am eternally grateful for you, thank you:

Allison Caso
Faith Wong
Jannette Carranza
Jessica Jin
Tonia Liu
Bridget Lee Sang
Pablo Arango
Rachel Johnson
Abigail Dunker
Grace Li
Sophie Naccarato
Wendy Lin
Yumei Li
Shurui Zhang
Chloe Chong
Vibin Ravi
Natalie Truong
Jenny Gong
Julia Yang
Carley Stafford
William Zhao
Jathin Belede
Tina Zeng
Sofia Murillo
Kyle Wang
Samuel Yang
Nina Mu
Clayton Xu
Ashley Zuercher
Fangyu Zhang
Macy Riley
Hugo Salazar-Vasquez

Demetrio Garcia
Angela Nguyen
Joseph Escobar
Tara Ollivier
Thomas Mahieu
James Wang
Benjamin Chong
Sin-Yu Shana Liu
Katrina Mohindroo
Lauren Turney
Brooke Dorsett
Rachel Zhu
Daniel Xiao
Nancy Yang
Macy Miller
Xintang Wang
Frances Wang
Doyeon Lee
TianTian Pan
Xingmei Diao
Yishan Dong
Chuanbo Zheng
Yuk Chen
Yan Xu
Tao gang
Shirley Tang
Ruilian Gao
Hua Yuan
Ran Wang
Xiqun Wei
Yan Dong
Achutha Srinivasan

Chen Liying
Elias Garibay
Katherine Xie
Logan Beltran
Eric Koester
Courtney Rinehart
Catherine Cai
Ruben Ramos
Christopher Harris
Dionis Rodriguez
Michael Bailey
Long Cheng
Guolong Zhang
ChihYu Chang

Pei-Yin Tai
Jonathon Dudgeon
Zein Tao
Elizabeth Xu
Gavin Wong
Carrie Xi
Gloria Xie
Anna Wong
Zoe Kika
Hudson River
Renee Lutz
Rebecca Xu
Austin Chan
Chen Jungang